To Mark:

all the best, big for everything.

text marked * on page 63 is completely unintentional).

go safe, go well — McDowell.

dec. 31, '93.

Good luck, Cyril. We'll miss you — but see you in Benny's on St Patrick's Day. And it's your round!

Love, Lindy xx

Dedicated with love and gratitude
to Caroline
who knew the Antrim Road
and was aware of the Hammer

Farewell to the Hammer

◆ to the ◆

A Shankill Boyhood

◆ John Young Simms ◆

WHITE ROW

The White Row Press

First published 1992 by
the White Row Press
135 Cumberland Road, Dundonald
Belfast BT16 OBB

This book has received assistance from the
Cultural Traditions Group of the Community Relations Council,
and the Arts Council of Northern Ireland

Cover: detail from
Passing the City Hall during a recruiting march
by William Conor
Ulster Museum, Belfast

Illustrations: William Clarke

Typesetting by Island Publications
Printed by The Universities Press Ltd

A catalogue record for this book is available
from the British Library

ISBN 1 870132 55 6

Farewell to the Hammer

◆ to the ◆

A Shankill Boyhood

◆ John Young Simms ◆

WHITE ROW

The White Row Press

Preface

This is an autobiographical work of high quality. It combines acute observation with a clarity of writing rare in the genre. The book, particularly in the first chapters, has such compressed recollection that each tale swells in the mind, like grain in water, until the reader finds it necessary to pause, and savour its taste, and go back over it again, before moving on the short distance to the next.

The Hammer was the name given to the streets that bordered the four sides of the swings in Ariel Street, midway along Agnes Street. Like so many similar districts the derivation of the name is now lost in time's haze; the author gives one explanation, involving football hacking, blood on the ground, and an earlier title, Sledgehammer Park, but there is a Belfast thud to the word that perfectly fits the Hammer, and this book conveys perfectly the hard times through which the writer walked, listening, watching, storing memories that are now set down here, with a rare purity, for all time.

There were Jews in the area, poor Jews, of Lithuanian extraction, families who fled persecution, and we can only wonder at the crushing weight of the pressures that led these unfortunate refugees, in the early part of the century, to regard the Hammer and its surrounding streets as a place of refuge. In John Young Simms' growing up years the streets also saw First War men maimed and gassed and shell shocked, and how they lived, and what they said and thought, the Jews and the men from the trenches, is here, on the record: a new annal is created.

The humour in these pages is the humour of the poor, the

pedigreed hungry, imprisoned in the city: 'The willicks in Greencastle are the best in the country, and I don't give a damn what anybody says about sewage.' These words could have been spoken in the twenties in Ringsend in Dublin, or Shandon Street in Cork, but they were said in Belfast, and plucked in their essence by a gifted plucker. In the space of a dozen pages three people hang themselves, but in the midst of such horror, Peter Fleming, 'who trailed the Hammer selling cod, herring, and dulse' gets drunk every Saturday, wraps his cap around his fist, and smashes every pane of glass in his house.

John Young Simms has been writing well for many years, and it shows in this his longest work to date. The book covers the years until he became a young man; it is so densely storied that, if he'd wanted, he could have filled it out and limited it to his school years, and his readers would still have been well content. So we can rejoice that what he has given us is not just memories and snippets, but a mother lode, a seam of rich, sad, funny, remembering: a lovely story, well told.

Sam McAughtry
Comber 1992

1

Before the bulldozers moved in I suppose the best way to help an enquiring stranger find the district known as the Hammer would have been to advise him to get to Ariel Street, midway along Agnes Street, and once there to look out for the large railed square known as 'the swings.' No one ever gave this patch of tarmac the grandiose title of playground. This was 'the swings', and the streets that bordered its four spiked sides almost perfectly described the Hammer.

And if the stranger asked how the area had come to get such a peculiar name, he would have been told that a football team called Crownville had once played on the dusty piece of ground where Hemsworth Square School now stands, and that they were such a pack of hackers that the ground was often left stained with blood after matches. Then some wit called the playing field Sledgehammer Park, which over time was shortened to the Hammer, and so the little streets surrounding, with their one roomed houses and their outside toilets and watertaps behind the front door forever after bore the name of the Hammer.

As a young child in the middle 1920s I lived in one of those streets, Fortingale Street, which ran from Agnes Street before twisting like a dog's hind leg onto the Old Lodge Road. Half-a-dozen houses had been demolished just before this twisting turn, and the derelict ground ran behind our house. Known to all and sundry as 'the waste', it was also a short cut to the football pitch and to Malvern Street, and the Shankill Road beyond. And on the waste on the twelfth day of July the singers would sing, the drummers would drum and the dancers would dance. Here, too, hard men stripped to their trousers and fought one another until they dropped down battered and exhausted.

s I moved slowly to the edge of my own yard wall I could hear voices coming from the backyard next door. Mrs Crawford lived there with her daughter Jenny who was slightly older than myself. She was a widow for Mr Crawford had been killed in an accident aboard a cargo boat when he worked as a merchant seaman.

Jenny was laughing and there were sounds of splashing water. This made me very curious so I raised up my arms and grasped the top of the low crumbling wall and heaved myself up to get a better view of what was going on.

The girl was standing up naked in a zinc bath and her mother was sponging down her back. My eyes popped in amazement for I had never beheld a naked girl in my life before. I gazed long at her body until Jenny spotted me peering over the wall. She started screaming like mad and the pigeons flew from the roofs in frantic haste, and with one hand to the upper part of her body and the other hand placed lower down she howled, 'Mammy, mammy, oh mammy!' Her mother looked up and gave a shout. 'Get off that bloody wall!' and she flung the wet sponge at my face.

Later that night there was to be a solemn discussion on the big steps of Blenheim Street School. It was a good place to congregate for the steps were wide and the deep arch over the doorway gave shelter in bad weather.

'I'm telling you Jenny Crawford is a cripple, for I saw her!'

'What makes you say that?' asked Garret who was in second standard and older than the rest of the gang.

I remember looking around as if fearing some outsider might hear and then replying in a loud whisper, 'I saw all of her for she was naked.'

'You mean to tell us that you saw her with no clothes on at all?' asked Wossie Hamilton.

'I tell you,' said I, 'I saw her in the bath with no clothes on and she had these big lumps on her chest and there was nothing between her legs.'

I... heaved myself up to get a better view...

'Maybe her father brought back a plague,' volunteered Jim Black.

'Ay, maybe you're right,' said Garret. 'It must be an awful pity of Jenny to have lumps and things missing like that.'

'All the same,' I answered back, 'you'd wonder why the doctors didn't cut the lumps off. They looked terrible!'

Dropping down quickly off the wall that day I hoped Mrs Crawford wouldn't run into my father and start yapping about me climbing on yard walls. However such thoughts disappeared when I came across a halfpenny lying amongst the stones. Drunks often used the back walls as an urinal and now and again the odd coin would also fall. Picking it up I made my way to the little shop owned by Mrs McKendrick.

The shop sat at the end of Fortingale Street and I was entranced with the place; especially with a faded postcard that occupied a corner of the window. It showed the picture of a woman dressed in the long skirts of the period standing with tears flowing down her cheeks. In the background was an army sergeant with an arm upraised about to hurl a grenade, whilst soldiers were scrambling out from a trench in the face of exploding shells and bullets. Across the top of the card was the legend: *For Men must Fight and Women must Weep.* I was convinced that it must be a photograph of Mrs McKendrick and her husband because she was always called 'Missus' and there was no man in the shop, so the way I looked at it, he must have been killed in the War.

I stood at the window and looked searchingly at the card. I never wearied of this and thought that Mr McKendrick must have been a very brave man to be standing there with all those bullets and shells whistling around him. I knew of course some of the men from around the streets had been in a fight called the Somme. There were men who were blind or with one eye or one arm or one leg. I had seen another man who had no legs, and the trousered stumps were covered by a kind of leathern apron and there were pads of red rubber on his hands. I used to watch fascinated as the man negotiated footpaths on his laborious way down the Old Lodge Road, shoving himself along with his hands. Someone told me that this man sat outside the GPO in Royal Avenue. The men I was most scared of were the shell-shocked. There was a man who would be walking along quite normally one minute, then the next he would be waving his arms wildly and yelling gibberish.

There were times when I would have stood for hours at Boundary Street corner where some of these men gathered. They now had no work and often no decent clothes to wear. They recalled horrible experiences. They seemed never to have left the War. I would stand there and drink in their talk.

hen I walked into Mrs McKendrick's shop the little woman with tinges of grey in her hair was standing behind the counter.

'Lamp oil, John?' she asked.

'No, Mrs McKendrick, I want a halfpenny's worth of Uncle Sam's Chewing Nuts.' These little toffee-covered nuts coated in sugar were my favourite sweets. As they were put into a paper poke for me I scrutinised the container that had the word PARAFFIN painted on it. It was a word I could never remember how to spell, although I came in often enough for a pint of it to light the lamps in our house. No one had electric light, and quite a few even had no gas for lighting or cooking.

Jim Black was walking past as I left the shop. Jim was my best pal and we were seldom out of one another's company. He hardly ever got called by his christian name; it was usually just Blackie.

'Hey boy,' he called to me. 'Where did you get the money for the sweets?'

'Found a halfpenny on the waste a little while ago. Want one?'

'What are they?'

'Uncle Sam's Chewing Nuts.'

'Now they're wee. What about a couple?'

As we walked up the street Blackie remarked. 'Did you hear about the witches' house?'

I asked him what about the witches' house.

'It's going to be pulled down this afternoon,' he answered.

'And who's going to pull it down?' I wanted to know.

'My ma said that the City Hall people were getting it pulled down because it was dangerous.'

'I'll see you around at the waste then after I get my dinner,' I told him.

At the waste men were bringing out ropes from a wooden building that housed the local drumming club. It was in here that practice was carried out on the Lambeg drums, the huge drums that thundered every twelfth day of July.

Tommy Bell seemed to be in charge. He was the man who would whitewash yard walls for a meal and a bottle of stout. He went over to the closed door of the crumbling old brick house that stood forlorn in the middle of the waste. Its windows were practically all gone, with pieces of sacking and cardboard filling up the gaps. Two old sisters lived in the hovel, eking out a precarious living by sewing and altering hand-me-downs belonging to the poorest.

Lots of people were gathered there, including half my class from school. I was there with Wossie, Garret, Blackie, Gouldie, Young, Murray, and Galway. Each and everyone of us believed firmly that the old sisters were witches, that they could work magic, and that no way would they ever let the house be demolished.

Tommy Bell was arguing with one of the women at the door.

'You've been well warned. Both of you have to leave right now'.

All of us pushed our way nearer to the door so that we could hear better.

'But the cats mister, what about the cats?'

'You've five minutes to get them out,' said big Tommy.

Then the men walked round the grimy old house pulling a rope after them. They started to tighten up the rope until both ends met at the door. 'Hurry up,' shouted big Tommy. 'Hurry up or we'll pull the damn place round you!'

The two old women came out. They were weeping. Some cats were mewing after them and everybody became quieter as they watched. They had several baskets in their hands and far from looking witchy they looked lonely and unwanted.

Big Tommy raised his whistle as the men tightened up the rope, then he ordered the crowd to move back. He blew the whistle and then shouted, 'Heave men, heave!' and like the participants in a tug-of-war the men pulled and strained, and slowly, ever so slowly, the walls started to cave in and slates fell and the old chimney crashed down. Then with a roar and in a tremendous cloud of dust the whole place collapsed.

There was cheering and clapping from the kids and then as the dust began to settle a cat was seen pushing desperately at the bricks. It had a kitten in its mouth and there was blood all over them. The sisters left their baskets down and ran crying to the animals and lifted them. There was an agony in the eyes of the evicted women. Blackie turned to me and said, 'I didn't think witches could cry.'

There was another time I would see the witches. Shortly after they had been turned out of the old house on the waste ground my mother took me down to one of the Scotch Halls in Christopher Street at the lower end of the Shankill Road. I never knew why some of these houses were called Scotch Halls; perhaps their echoing stone halls compared with halls of a similar kind in Scotland.

The old sisters had a room in one of these houses and my mother had taken me there to have trousers made. In the rented room there was a bed with brassy ends. It was covered with coats and cloth, and there were also several hard-backed chairs and a plain wooden table. The women were very polite and most particular in the measuring of the cloth to be used for the trousers. Although I was still a little frightened of them, the awful scene of their eviction was still imprinted upon my mind. There were no cats in this place, no shocked bewildered little animals and no grey-haired witches standing bitterly sobbing. But deep down I knew they couldn't be witches for as Blackie had said, 'Witches don't cry.'

 few days later I was poking around the waste hoping to find a marble or the stub of a pencil amongst the discarded fish and chip papers. I was in no hurry for I was on holiday from Blenheim Street School, and in any case I had to be careful amongst the glass and sharp stones for I was in my bare feet. Sometimes I was lucky, like the morning I had found a box filled to the top with cigarette cards. There was a complete set of wild flowers and a set of English football players. My heart had thumped madly when I discovered what was inside the box, and I was to be the envy of all the kids in the neighbourhood until I eventually lost them all playing blowsies.

Another great find had been a handbag containing insurance policies and a purse holding several rings and sets of keys. When I showed the bag to my father he went along with me to the address printed on one of the policies. It was Cliftonpark Avenue, a very posh place then where teachers and doctors had big houses, and it wasn't too far from Fortingale Street. My father was hopeful that I would be well rewarded.

A maid brought her mistress to the front door and after the lady had thoroughly searched through the handbag she went back into the house telling my father and I to wait.

Then the maid returned and handed over tuppence. My father was mad about the meanness of the old skinflint's reward, and there and then I vowed that there would be no more returning of finds.

ummer was all over the land. From the heights of the Divis mountains, where on a clear day moving specks could be seen that were the movements of cows and sheep, right down to the fields surrounding the Ballygomartin Road, right down the Shankill Road, and down the cobbled streets of the Hammer there was summer. The warm summer days passed quickly, taken up with games and simple joys which, to those ignorant of the lives of the poor, might have seemed bizarre and even wicked.

Thread was tied to the legs of bluebottles and youngsters shouted in excitement as the flies moved in frantic circles up and away towards the black slates of the houses. Mice were caught by plucking them from the jaws of astonished cats, or by angling a piece of sausage on the end of a string down a hole in a bedroom floor or beside a broken skirting board. Like Eskimos over an icehole, the angler patiently waited for a bite and when it came there was the quick haul back and the grab. Most times it was a successful grab for the mice of the poor were usually hungry and loath to let go of any morsel. Then threads were attached to their tails and the tiny animals were walked as one would walk a dog, and were given names like Flash and Speedy, becoming in time so tame that they would sit up and beg for food.

We also enjoyed great times at the Shore Road municipal dump, where enormous pools of murky water would gather after showers of rain. We had found this rude marino set amidst mountains of smouldering rubbish during one of our visits to Greencastle to gather willicks. It was a case of foraging around until an old tin bath or an old dust bin was unearthed and then one had the choice of a length of wood and one was off on a voyage across faery seas of adventure:

> *Oh where will I get a skeely skipper*
> *To sail this new ship of mine?*

The tiny animals were walked as one would walk a dog...

Then there were the rows over seamanship:

'I don't care what you say John. My da told me...'

'You can't have a tide coming in on just a big puddle of water.'

'My da says the moon pulls all the water in the world.'

'His head's cut; you'll be a long time in this before the tide comes in.'

 didn't mind the end of the holidays, for I was fond of school. My school for some unfathomable reason was called Blenheim Street School, though no Blenheim Street existed anywhere. I had been going since before I was four years of age.

I will never forget my first day. It had been a morning

given over to sleety rain and gusting winds. My mother dragged me bawling along the streets with one hand, the other clutching her black shawl to prevent it blowing off her body. When we arrived I and a lad by the name of Willie Nelson were left to dry by a coal fire, but it was a long time before my tears dried for I was frightened and miserable.

The teacher was a Miss Moore; in fact there were no married ladies on the teaching roll in those days. Miss Moore was a stout lady whose gentle appearance belied a no-nonsense attitude. She was mistress in charge of over forty fidgety, restless boys and girls, divided into junior and senior infants.

After roll-call Miss Moore would get everyone to hold out their hands to make sure that they had been washed. Most of the pupils usually had their hands and faces well washed, but the few who had not were made to go out into the school yard and splash cold water over themselves from an old leaking faucet, sagging from a brick wall.

Insolence or bad manners were not tolerated, but although these were the days when the cane was frequently employed to instil morals into wayward children, Miss Moore never used it. Instead she would put offenders over her knees and administer a few hearty thumps with her hand upon the backside.

One morning the senior class was being instructed in naming colours and for this purpose Miss Moore had gone laboriously around the desks placing a red, yellow, green and blue strand of wool before each child. Whilst her back was turned I twisted round to the desks behind me and blew my breath at the pieces of wool lying there. They went everywhere.

There were gasps from the tiny pupils at this act of mischief and immediately there was a shuffling and stooping in an effort to rearrange the wool. Miss Moore became aware of the commotion and straightening up she glared around her to discover Lily Frampton attempting to sort out the little bits of wool.

'What are you doing standing up?' demanded Miss Moore in a severe tone.

'The wool blew away Miss,' said Lily.

'Oh,' retorted the teacher, coming up now to the desk.

'And what blew it away?'

The girl hesitated.

'Well?' insisted Miss Moore.

'It just blew, Miss.'

'And who did the blowing?'

I sat tight in my desk. I was waiting for my name and already saw myself across Miss Moore's knees with big whacks descending upon my bottom.

'Who blew the wool all over the place Lily?'

The little blonde girl looked down on the floor and in a frightened voice said, 'I don't know.'

'Very well,' said Miss Moore, 'that means either you were not paying attention or you are lying. Please come out to the front.'

'But Miss...' pleaded the girl.

'Come out this instant.'

The whole class sat in silence whilst Lily Frampton's skirt was pulled up and she was smacked across the bottom. Lily never uttered a word and I didn't look while the punishment was taking place. I was too young to be over-concerned with my guilt but I knew I had done something wrong, and that little incident of Lily bravely accepting the blame for something that was not of her making has always stayed with me. Every time I met her afterwards I tried to cover my embarrassment by greeting her with 'Hello, Lily Smacks.'

In the afternoons we would sing while Miss Moore accompanied us on an ancient harmonium. She had two favourite songs, one of them a sad song about a little flower girl:

> *Underneath the gaslight's glitter,*
> *Stands a weary, forlorn girl.*
> *Heedless of the cold winds bitter,*
> *As they round about her whirl.*

We would put everything we had into this song, and as we stood by our desks, some of us very ragged looking in hand-me-down clothes and a few of the boys in their bare feet, the pathos of the simple words and the sight of singing children

so nurtured in poverty occasionally made even the redoubtable
Miss Moore pull out her handkerchief and rub a tear from
her eye.

2

The fat man was standing on a horse-drawn brake. His voice was raised and there was perspiration upon his red face. 'Vote for me and these slums will go; I tell you, these slums will go! No more watertaps behind the front door, no more outside toilets, no more crumbling wet walls. You'll have bathrooms and hot running water and gardens,' and here the voice rose almost to croaking, 'I tell you, these slums will come crashing down like the walls of Jericho when you give me your vote! Vote in your thousands tomorrow!'

The crowds cheered, the drums rolled and the dogs barked, and oul' Jimmy White threw his cap into the air and shouted, 'No surrender!' The shawled women clapped their hands. Union Jacks waved furiously and people called out, 'Bully oul' Jimmy!' And then, half-heartedly at first, but soon to develop into full-throated song the crowd roared out:

> *We'll fight for no surrender,*
> *We'll fight when duty calls.*
> *With heart and hand and sword and shield,*
> *We'll guard old Derry's walls.*

The orator raised a hand, using the other to mop the inside of his starched white collar with a hugh handerchief. He was immaculately dressed in a dark suit with a gold Albert slung across his waistcoat, which served to enhance a sizeable paunch. Voice breaking, he bellowed: 'The men and women of the Hammer have sense, they are not easily gulled by their enemies; they are not going to be dragged into the land of

Popery. They are sons and daughters of great people; people who fought dearly for Ulster, and now like their forebears they are going to prove that they have fire in their bellies. They are going to vote for right!'

The crowd roared its enthusiasm as the potbellied man sat down:

> *Do you think that I would let*
> *An oul Fenian cat*
> *Destroy my leaf of a lily-o.*

I watched the whole show. I had been thrilled by the shouts, by the band, by the flag waving and the singing. I knew those songs well enough, but I was curious about the Popery bit, about the place called the Border. My father was standing beside me at our front door. 'Why is it da that the Catholics are always fighting?'

'Och son,' said he, 'they are still flaming mad because we gave them a good hiding at the Boyne. It gets their goat up to be reminded of them days, especially when we sing the songs.' I got no more history out of him. All that had gone. The songs were all he knew.

The windows on the north side of Blenheim School overlooked a large portion of derelict ground. It was a grand place for the kids and during school holidays was all sorts of things to many of the pupils. For some it was a short cut over to Eton Street; for others it was Windsor Park or Wembley. To me, as a boy of ten, it was Treasure Island and indeed, sad to say, it had its Ben Gunns and its Long John Silvers making their miserable way across accumulations of wine bottles, weeds and rubble. Henderson made a tent out of potato sacks on that derelict ground, Haslett put one up also, so did Greenlees. Overnight it became a settlement, a tiny oasis populated by half of the kids from around the Hammer, and how enchanted I had felt when, while clearing a spot to insert a tent pole, I came across a bag filled with marbles, whilst my pal Blackie found two pennies.

Everyone had to bring a potato and a piece of firewood

and then Henderson and the other bigger fellows made a pot of stew with the spuds, some onions and a hunk of corned beef. What bliss those nights were, what adventures we had on Treasure Island, and of course there was no rain in those far off days of childhood. Or so it seemed.

And just as at scouts' or boys' brigade camps everyone gathered around a huge fire and sang the hours away. It being the July holidays songs like *Dolly's Brae* and *The Green Grassy Slopes Of The Boyne* always got an airing, the Jewish kids from Fortingale Street and Bristol Street singing just as lustily as the rest. Their destitute parents had in the main come over from Lithuania to escape the tyranny of the Czar. One of the boys, Davy Isaacs had a powerful voice for such a frail body and he would lift us all right over Dolly's Brae. Abie Sergie was another good singer and he would fill the nights with ballads about Tennessee and sweet old Georgia.

Then came the 'Goodness gracious, what's happening over there?' from Mr Smyth the headmaster of Blenheim School that signalled its end. One day on looking across from the classroom window he saw the men on Treasure Island digging and hammering, carting and tipping. There were stacks and stacks of corrugated iron sheets and wooden and concrete posts, and men with bowler hats and men with bits of paper and pencils, and Treasure Island, from that morning, began to disappear. There were walls of metal going up and walls of brick and everyone in class was confused and desolate.

Finally a huge biscuit depot enveloped the whole of the precious ground. Everybody had to listen to the noise of vans and lorries on solid tyres rumbling in and out of a building that everyone hated the sight of. Never again would we have those nights of singing *Swanee, Dolly's Brae* and *Onward Christian Soldiers*. Never again would we taste stew like the stuff that was made in the big black pot on the Island.

round this time I used to make a daily visit to see Cathy Scanlon. She was about my age and lived in my street. Cathy was bedridden with tuberculosis, a disease that also afflicted one of her sisters and her mother. The father worked in Linfield Mill, a place I too would work in, engaged in the heaviest work performed in the mill, which was that of the yarn hawker.

Cathy was lying as usual in bed in a small back room. Flies swarmed about the house in dozens, for fresh air was then held to be a cure for tuberculosis, so the windows and doors lay wide open. A sticky length of flypaper dangled from the ceiling. It was almost black with the corpses of flies. Her mum was sitting by an empty grate coughing and spluttering, and taking the odd pinch of snuff.

'Mrs Scanlon,' said I, 'the voting man says he is going to get our houses knocked down.'

Mrs Scanlon was far from pleased.

'They're not going to knock the place down now, surely?'

'Yes. But we're going to get new houses, with baths and washhand basins.'

She stared at me with a look of what I now know was probably sympathy.

Inside, Cathy, gasping for air, tried to tell me that she was sure she would live until she was sixteen, and be able to skip, something she had never been able to do. There were flies on the walls and on the blanket. I told her that I would bring her a couple of lizards from the Forth River. They were good for catching flies and they wouldn't bite her.

Tuberculosis was a real scourge. Four of my friends died of it before reaching adulthood. Poor Cathy did not see her eleventh birthday.

One of my delights in those days was to ride on Mercer's breadvan, a closed, flat-roofed, horse-drawn vehicle built on two very large wheels, its interior filled with sliding shelves holding soda farls, fruit cakes and 'cuttin' bread. My da preferred this bread, which was actually bread that was a little stale, for the fresh kind gave him indigestion.

One thing that my da was good at was putting a letter together, and he was much in demand when it came to communicating with officialdom. People would come from near and far to have letters written or get advice on dole matters, or to trace dates of birth when seeking a pension. He always had time for the different characters who came to his door. He was also a great admirer of individuals like Tommy Henderson and Arthur Trew, working class men who had attained a certain eminence in local affairs. He was a seasonal worker in McClinton's seed mill in Divis Street, and a collecting steward for the Irish Transport Union that had its office in Corporation Street.

Another side to my father was his knowledge of the whereabouts of almost every park, avenue, road, court, mews and alley in Belfast. He knew where the shortest, and where the longest street was. He knew that Woodvale Park was opened in 1888, and that the mayor, Sir James Haslett who was to open it, failed to turn up. He knew that Alexander Park was opened in 1887 but had to be closed again until later in the year because of vandalism, when it was then opened by the park ranger who just strolled forward and swung open the gate. That was my da, the memory man, the local scribe and father confessor.

Wee Mrs Gault came to see him one day. She was flustered. 'Ye see Sammie, I have these forms from a solicitor and he wants to know this and that and where I was baptised. To tell you the truth Sammie, I don't know if I was baptised or not.'

'Right, Maggie,' he began, peering into the first of the intimidating forms...

Shortly afterwards Mrs Gault received a cheque, the amount of which in those days was equal to about eight years wages of an average man. Little knots of people could be seen at doorways, at corners, in Higginson's shop in Fortingale Street, at the entrance to Finlay's pawn on the Old Lodge Road, all talking about the legacy left Mrs Gault.

'She's nearly a millionaire Susie.'

'An uncle in Australia left her all his money.'

'God knows but aren't some people lucky.'

'Imagine an oul' doll like that rollin' in money.'

The Gaults went on the spree. No holds barred. For months the *Malvern Arms* on the corner of Malvern Street was a Mecca for the red biddy fraternity, con men, oilcloth salesmen, ladies-of-the-night, down-and-outs, and winos from far and near. The stout flowed. There were tiffs, squabbles and stripped-to-the-waist fights. There were banquets on pigs' feet, elder and tripe. There was health onto His Majesty, and sickness onto death. Mr and Mrs Gault were the first, and just about the last, of the Hammer's big spenders.

Then both of them were conned into buying a small farm near Hillsborough – a farm, and the Gaults had hardly ever been in close contact with a Brussels sprout all their lives!

Their eldest son asked me to accompany him one wet day to see Rose Farm, as it was called, and we set off from the old bus station in North Street. We found it after a lot of trouble, and it lay glistening like Lough Henny in the watery sunlight. We had passed it, but it was so waterlogged that we had been certain it was an inland lake.

My recollections of Rose Farm in the aftertimes didn't consist of roses, or stooks of corn, or fields of barley. What I would remember was the lined face of the man who lived in the farm cottage, and his terribly shy daughter, with her long wild auburn hair and her plain, soiled dress.

But we got a good welcome at the cottage, with tea out of thick mugs and soda farls for the two of us.

'It's been a damp year the year,' said the man. We agreed.

'When will we be able to grow potatoes and barley?' asked young Gault.

'Oh, that rests in God's hands.'

'Can cows be raised on the farm?' I asked.

'Sure son,' said the man, 'cows would be hardy bastes.'

But there was neither a cow on Rose Farm, nor fields of waving barley, nor even a spud during the short period it was owned by the Gaults.

Meanwhile, the sad binge continued. Mr Gault discovered he had a taste for cigars. Mrs Gault indulged in snuff. Quite often they came home to their little kitchen house in the Hammer sitting up on a jaunting car, and often as not it was a job to get Mr Gault down for he kept arguing with the jarvey and saying, 'I'll buy the damn thing off you.'

And then after six months the spree stopped; the river of booze dried up and hangers-on disappeared, and the little pub reverted to its usual pint-of-Guinness men. There were no more jaunting cars, no more cigars. Instead there was the enveloping again of the chronic poverty, the cheap margarine, the twice boiled tea-leaves. In other words, things returned to normal. Like sojourners emerging from a wilderness of tears they had greedily embraced the sweet taste of honey. But now the boom was over, the money gone. My da never really faulted them. The reward for his good services had been ten shillings and a bottle of lemonade.

hen I first realised that I could read intelligently, or at any rate make sense of the words in the *Funny Wonder* comic, I felt like old Archimedes who had raced down the street shouting Eureka. I wasn't lying in a bath when I made this discovery, I was lying in bed and found with a shock that I could understand the yarn about Cowboy Charlie and his horse. Previously I had depended upon the cartoons of Captain Codseye or Weary Willie and Tired Tim to titillate me, but now that I had read a whole story I was bursting with pride.

I tumbled and tossed in bed for most of that night, thrilled at this new-found proficiency, and itching to tell my companions about this great feat. Eventually sleep came and with it dreams of Cowboy Charlie's horse and other horses as well; big prancing stallions snorting and shaking handsome heads. I galloped over dusty plains, handling my steed with ease, and watching the Red Indians quail whenever I showed up on the horizion. And thus on that eventful night years ago I had made another discovery: I was fond of horses.

I put it all down to the old breadserver, and the way he let me guide his horse Sam round the streets of the Hammer. As I sat upon my perch in charge of this magnificent beast, with my feet pressed against the slanted iron foot-plate that lent purchase to ones legs when checking the horse, I could have shouted with delight.

And no doubt that is how my great desire arose. Whilst travelling around Malvern Street and Belgrave Street on the breadcart the thought had sometimes struck me – how would I cope if I came across a runaway horse? In my mind's eye I could visualise myself being fleetfooted and brave enough to stop a horse that had been frightened into dashing down the Shankill Road. I knew I would grab the dangling reins that were hanging from a slobbering mouth with one hand, while my other hand went round the great beast's neck. And even though I am being trailed along the square setts and there are sparks flying from the agonised wheel rims, I somehow bring the great brute to a halt. The big animal snorts and trembles but I sooth it, and its bloodshot eyes gradually clear. Then I hear another noise. This time it is the sound of a cheering, clapping crowd. A policeman pats me on the back and puts my name in his notebook, and I walk away feeling ten feet tall. As tall as Cowboy Charlie.

 o greatly did this desire to stop a runaway horse impinge itself upon my imagination that I walked around the Shankill, the Crumlin and the Old Lodge roads eyeing the horses moving hither and thither, ready to spring, to dart out, to grab the reins or to jump onto a heaving back and become as big a hero as the lad who saved Holland by plugging the dyke with his finger.

It was not to be however. How fate makes nonsense of dreams! Tommy McMurray was a cousin of mine who lived in Paris Street. He stopped a runaway horse in York Street. It was a horse that pulled a breadvan too, belonging to Warwick's bakery. He had clambered up the rear of the van, then got onto the animal's back and pulled it up. The incident was in all the papers and the bakery manager told him he could have a job anytime with the company. But Tommy was already working and refused the offer. He wasn't even looking for runaway horses either; he was only doing an errand. Some people are just born to be great.

 here was a shop at the corner of Langford Street owned by a family by the name of Mercer, and the letters on the gable wall spelt out that they sold mangles and repaired rollers. The two boys of the family went to Blenheim Street School and the younger one was a pretty good singer. He had also a pretty good jaw for one afternoon I tried to show him how a boxer knocked out an opponent by hitting the point of the jaw. I made a terrible mistake and nearly broke my hand when the haymaker I swung at him –

We were the envy of the street.

and which was supposed to miss – landed instead. Young Mercer staggered but didn't go down. He took it in good part though, and seemed perfectly convinced.

Anyway, after saving for about six months my father was able to buy a reconditioned mangle from Mercer for ten shillings. It was delivered by horse and cart belonging to a Mr Irvine; he was a trader in oilcloth around the district and all he charged for the delivery was a pint of Guinness. His horse was really part of the family for when the day's work was done it would be unharnessed and then led through the kitchen out into the back yard where it was stabled.

To me that mangle was a thing of beauty. Out in her small yard my mother would do the washing over her wooden scrubbing board with a bar of Sunlight soap. The scrubbing board would be placed in a galvanised tin tub of hot water and the clothes would be rubbed up and down the corrugated ribs of the board. This was murder on the knuckles and often my mother's became cracked and bleeding.

I loved helping with the mangling, and as far as my childish strength would allow I would place shirts and stockings between the wooden rollers and turn the iron wheel that rotated them. Out the water would be squeezed and then my mother would hang the articles out to dry. We were the envy of the street and many a neighbour would come to our door asking if they could have their blankets wrung.

One day Mrs Irvine suggested that I could mangle her blankets for a penny and I jumped at the chance. I had to ask my elder brother Sam to help me, for blankets were a tough proposition for one little boy. We spread them out, then inserted one end between the rollers. It was a hard grind and it took our combined strength to rotate the wheel. Halfway through the operation Sam left the wheel whilst he untangled a bit of uneveness and wham, back came the wheel! The handle hit me on the point of the jaw and sent me sprawling across the yard.

Up in the Mater Hospital the questions came... 'Who did you say hit him Mr Simms?'

'It was a mangle doctor.'

'A mongol?'

'A mangle.'

'Mr Simms, are you trying to say mongol?'

'No doctor I'm not. He was turning a mangle when the handle flew back and banged him on the jaw.'

I was too young then to be bothered overmuch about divine retribution and of course had no knowledge of the practice of sticking pins into dolls – or mangles. Possibly Willie Mercer wasn't the kind to indulge in evil thoughts about that unintentional fist in his face, but nonetheless it all seemed a bit queer to me.

After the Mercers left the district the premises became a fish supper saloon and many a fourpenny supper I had along with a thruppeny bottle of lemonade brewed at the Cromac Springs plant. This was of course when I became a worker, and on a Saturday night I felt almost exalted, spending, it seemed, like a millionaire whilst sitting at my meal in a tiny cubicle. Seven pence for the fish and chip supper and mineral, three pence for admittance to Big Joe's picture house on the Shankill Road and a fourpenny packet of Wild Woodbines to end the day. Opulence indeed!

3

his man came along in an effort to rescue the people of the Hammer from their sins. He wasn't going to march them over the Boyne. He had a more inviting place to go.

We're marching to Zion
Beautiful, beautiful Zion.
We're marching to Zion,
That beautiful city of God.

He was a great preacher, small and thin, and he worked in the shipyard: 'Come to the mercy seat, come while there is time. Move away from the black lips of hell and repent of your sins. The politicians cannot save you, nobody can save you, only the blood of the precious Lord!'

Blackie and I knelt at the mercy seat and were converted.

'Do you feel any different, Jim?'

'I think a wee bit.'

'I'm going to tell my ma. She's goodlivin' herself.'

'I think I'll wait a while before I tell anybody.'

'We'll have to stop going up to the Forth River to catch the spricks.'

'Why's that?'

'Well, they're all God's creatures. It wouldn't be right.'

All things bright and beautiful,
All creatures great and small.
All things wise and wonderful,
The Lord God made them all.

A mighty labour was begun and the little preacher started a soup kitchen. Collections were taken at gospel meetings and a couple of pounds of stewing meat were purchased from Bowman's, the high class butcher on the Shankill Road. Harry Wright got converted too. Because he was in the scouts he got the job of making the soup, and he always insisted on obtaining the vegetables from Grays on the Old Lodge Road. So the hungry were fed. Oul' Jimmy White said there was never enough salt put in, and Mrs Kane said the vegetables were better out of Nixon's. The preacher would preach the gospel each night and often said that man could not live by bread alone. I felt encouraged by this directive for I always took plenty of soup.

During the weeks when I was at my most devout I used to open my Bible at random, and then closing my eyes I would jab a finger down upon some verse anticipating a great message would be vouchsafed me. Often I made a couple of jabs if the selection did not tally with my hopes. And thus by this hit and miss method of guidance I was directed by the Good Book to go into the world and preach the gospel.

A great sense of purpose had invaded my soul since being washed in the Blood. There would be no sinning for the next lot of years if it were within my power to stay on the straight and narrow path. In the meanwhile I proposed to read the Bible from start to finish. I composed little poems dealing with the evils of strong drink and stuck them up in public places, like the walls of libraries and on the front doors of pubs – without my signature of course.

I went to the Albert Hall on the Shankill and duly took the pledge to abstain from strong drink. I liked the Albert Hall because the superintendent, the Reverend Montgomery, really loved the people of the district. The Reverend organised parties for children, food parcels for the needy and the homeless, and ran a holiday home for multitudes of youngsters as well.

Standing on the crowded floor of the Albert Hall we yelled:

> *Dare to be a Daniel,*
> *Dare to stand alone.*

Dare to have a purpose firm
And dare to make it known.

It helped the ragged to ignore their rags and the ill-nourished to forget the constant pangs of hunger. And I did the Oliver Twist bit too. Once when I had been in the shouting, shoving, restless queue of children along with my younger brother, impatiently waiting for the iron gates to open and admit us, we had got close to the entrance. A couple of men then briefly closed the gates to stem the rush of the excited mob. Closed them right on my hand.

The pain was excruciating but my cries were hardly heard above the din of screaming youngsters. The men eventually realised what had happened and swiftly released my bruised and swollen hand. Meanwhile my brother had been pulled and pummelled so much that he had lost his place, and had been forced out onto the pavement, forlorn and weeping. As the hall soon filled, he and dozens of others could not be admitted.

'This way for the buns, boys,' – no girls mind you – and the boys would squeeze up the aisle towards several helpers who were doling out bags of buns to each as they passed along.

'Mister,' I said, 'could I have another Paris bun?'

'Another Paris bun lad? Whatever for?'

'For my brother mister. He couldn't get in.'

'Do you hear that Willie – he wants another bun for his brother.'

'You telling the truth boy?'

'I am mister.'

'Give him another bag, Joe,'

...and then my mother kissing me for bringing the buns back home and fussing over my swollen fingers.

wonder what sort of pillar of the church I would have become if Rachel Morrow had promised to go to darkest Africa with me. Rachel lived in Downing Street, and her mother had set up a small shop in their little kitchen house in an attempt to bring in a few extra pennies.

One day Rachel was standing at the corner of Downing

Street, standing against the gable wall with the big painting
of King William of Orange on his white horse crossing the
Boyne with his sword held high. She was surrounded by a
bevy of boys from Blenheim School and she was laughing and
chatting animatedly. A twinge of jealously started up within
me which was curiously fused with the awful feeling that
gorgeous Rachel was on the road to Hell. I stopped and
joined in the talk and when I judged the moment to be right,
I blurted out with intense evangelical fervour, 'Why don't
you get saved, and then when we leave school we can train for
the Mission Field.'

There was a stunned silence. Then Rachel squealed with
laughter. 'You mean,' she managed to say, 'to go out amongst
the black cannibals?'

Some of the smart alecs then joined in. 'Doctor Livingstone,
I presume?'

'Wouldn't you rather go as a lion tamer, John?'

'Remember the joke Rachel about the missionary who
kept smiling though he was tucked up in a cooking pot. The
cannibals were all sitting in a circle gazing at the pot when
the chief said, 'Why are you smiling, Mr Missionary?' and the
missionary replied, 'A watched pot never boils.'

Harry Wright was the first to break his conversion and I
felt rotten about it after the scout stopped coming to the
meetings. He had been teaching me how to make sheepshanks
and half hitches and I delighted in showing off my cleverness
at school. Then I called big Craig a pigeon-chested bugger
one day and broke my own conversion. But to cap it all the
preacher got arrested for embezzling the soup money, and
was given six months in Crumlin Road jail.

A blacksmith's shop opened in the former gospel hall and
I spent hours watching the horses being shod. The sparks
would fly from the anvil and the sweet smell of burning
hooves would waft all over the place. I liked the smell but
often wondered why the blacksmith didn't take down the red
banner from the side wall which had in big capital letters:
SAVED BY THE BLOOD. Oul' Jimmy White would come
around too for an hour. He hadn't much good to say about
the preacher – 'A fly boy thon. And his soup was rotten!'

hen there were the times on the Forth River. It was easy to get to the Forth through Woodvale Park. I was with Blackie and Rea on one of our fishing expeditions. We had glass jars and cloth nets punctured here and there with holes to allow the water to escape when sweeping through the river for spricks. And it always had to be black cloth for fish could see colours according to Peter Fleming, who trailed the Hammer selling cod, herrings and dulse. Every Saturday without fail Mr Fleming would come out of the *Busy Bee* pub and stagger the short distance to his house. Then, in a well practised ritual which never failed to fascinate me, he took off his cap, wrapped it around one fist, and then proceeded to smash every tiny pane in his window.

Woodvale cricket club was playing this lovely sunny afternoon and I stopped to see a few overs before continuing to the Forth. 'You two go ahead, I'll catch up,' I told my pals. Hundreds of people were sitting around on the grass watching this renowned team play. I sat at the edge of the huge crowd, carefully setting down my glass jar and net. I didn't know who the visiting team was that day and I knew far less a few minutes later. A big swing came across in my direction and the ball crashed against my forehead, knocking me out. My next recollection was of coming to in the pavilion dressing room surrounded by people anxiously looking into my eyes or feeling my pulse or rubbing liquid on my forehead. I felt a wee bit shaky for a while, but with the resilience of young years I was soon on my feet again.

'Where's my jar and net?'

'What are you talking about son?'

'My jar and net for catching spricks.'

These were found and with about two shillings in my pocket, mostly in coppers given to me by sympathisers, I was soon on my way, bursting to tell my pals how I had caused the big match at Woodvale Park to be temporarily suspended and, of course, to show off my lump.

he days slipped by in living and loving on those crowded Hammer back streets. And then there occurred a shocking event. The blacksmith was found hanging from a rope underneath the big banner that said, SAVED BY THE BLOOD. Harry Wright lived next door to the forge and came tearing round to our house that Sunday morning to tell the news. Harry had actually been inside the forge and had taken a good look at the poor man before a policeman had cuffed his ear and told him to get to hell out of it. But Harry knew the sort of knot that made up the noose on the rope and the blacksmith's face was blue.

We ran round to the shop where the crowd was pushing and shoving. All were staring at the big wooden gates which were now closed. The ambulance was there and Fat Joe the bobby was squeezing in and out through the small inset door, looking very important. Scotty the wino was leaning out of his upstairs window waving a bottle about, now and then putting it to his lips. He was a great lover of the red biddy. Then the blacksmith's body was carried out on a shutter covered by a blanket. Everyone stopped talking for a moment and I felt frightened as the shutter was lifted into the ambulance. Some woman close to me said he had been in a lot of debt. Someone else said he had been going around with another man's wife.

At that instant Scotty dropped his bottle and it struck a little girl on the head. She began screaming, the blood pouring down her face. 'Stop the flamin' ambulance!' a very sensible man shouted, and in no time at all everybody was shouting, 'Stop the ambulance for the wee girl!' Fat Joe had been following the ambulance on his bicycle and he fell off trying to dismount. This was too much for the onlookers and they mocked and jeered him. The ambulance driver put the girl into the vehicle along with her mother although the mother said she was scared to be so close to the blacksmith.

The things that shock the senses never seem to come singly. There was an old lady who on fine days would sit at the corner of her street on a wooden stool; her name was McMinn. One time a passing drunken women was having harsh words with her and when Mrs McMinn stood up this other woman lifted up the stool and hit her over the head with it. It fractured her scull but she regained her health very quickly and was soon back on her stool at the corner. Three weeks

after the blacksmith was buried she was found hanging from
a big nail on her scullery door. The stool was lying upturned
beneath her feet.

here was a fellow by the name of Robinson who lived
off Agnes Street. He had a job in the abattoir down by
the Belfast markets, and as we stood on the school
steps at night he would regale us with all sorts of frightfulness.
The girls would say, 'Oh, that's terrible!' But me, Craig and
Blackie would tighten our lips like hard men and say nothing
when he spoke of parting an animal's brains by probing their
mortal wounds with a cane. Rachel Morrow thought the
whole business was desperate, but Robinson replied she didn't
say that when she was eating a piece of jump steak out of
Bowman's.

Robinson could almost make one a vegetarian just by chatting.
None of the listeners knew anything about cows of course.
They were unknown animals. I knew a little about horses and
dogs, and I had helped to feed the pigs at the back of Caruth's
store in Downing Street. But we were all just a little scared of
cows. We'd seen things. You just couldn't trust them.

We lads had watched the cattle drovers blatter the cows
between the Queen's Bridge and the Albert Bridge as they
were being driven to the cross channel boats. Many a time we
had had to dash for our lives when all of a sudden a dozen or
so massive brutes would break away and come stampeding
and roaring and pointing their horns at us. Mind you we
weren't the only ones to sprint out of the way. Shop girls,
office workers and even men from the shipyard would scatter
like people demented when they broke.

One evening cattle brought the shipyard trams to a standstill.
A long row of these pneumonia boxes with their partially
open opposite ends was lined up on the tracks, loaded to
over capacity with workers clinging to every handhold, the
drivers impatiently stamping on the metal bars that activated
the gongs. Out jumped this old fellow of a conductor who
started banging some of the beasts on their rumps.

'Hey boy, lave them bastes alone!' shouted a red-faced
drover.

'Hey, boy, lave them bastes alone!'

'Lave them alone me backside!' retorted the conductor, his big moustache quivering, 'My car's late.'

He continued to thump one of the cows and the drover yelled again: 'Ye stick to yer job and I'll do mine.'

'I'm a country man,' spluttered the old lad, 'and I can handle bastes better than ye.' And just then the cow lifted its tail and covered him with foul, dark liquid. The tension broke, people doubled up with laughter. If there had been a photographer about it would have been the picture of the century.

Robinson was always inviting us down, so one morning Blackie and I went to the abattoir. There were men in rubber boots and there was blood all over the floor and carcasses hanging from hooks, and the men with the knives were slashing.

Cows were being tugged along on chain halters. They smelt the blood. They were crazy with fear and were mooing and pulling and stamping their feet, but there was no one there to help them, no one at all. A man put some kind of gun against an animal's head and it crashed to the floor of the pen. A rabbi felled another by drawing a knife across its throat.

Both of us felt sick and uneasy. A young woman at the exit door was drinking a glass of blood, for she was ill with anaemia, and was a ghastly white colour. Then we left that gory place and never went back.

4

I t was a wet blustery night and the wires strung from the telephone poles on the Antrim Road heaved and glistened like a shoal of fish stricken by fear. My mother in her shawl struggled in the whipping wind and at each intersection she would ask me, 'Is this it yet?' It was difficult in the darkening streets to distinguish the name of Kansas Avenue, for the name plates were high up on the walls of the corner houses. Rain trickled down my bare legs into my canvas shoes so that my feet made squelching noises when I walked. I wore no overcoat or jacket, only a crumpled grey jersey that clung wetly to my body. My mother was breathing heavily as she trudged along and her back was bent as she urged herself against the wind. When we reached the corner of Kansas Avenue she stood for a few moments to regain control of her breath and I stood beside her, waiting. Some of the windows in the avenue were lit up by coloured bulbs and candles, for this was Christmas Eve.

And so it was that we came to the door of Mr Peshkin the Jew. Most people in the Hammer area who got drapery on tick knew Mr Peshkin, for he had traded around the Hammer since he had been a young man. He was brisk and jovial, always smoking and always lumbered with a large heavy suitcase. The suitcase when opened revealed a treasure trove of shirts, vests, caps, dresses and blankets, made up in every possible colour. My mother had been paying him a shilling per week for six or seven years now for the family clothes. She was a good customer, a proud person, who would do without a meal rather than miss paying her tick money.

Mr Peshkin knew she was dependable and would have trusted her with any amount of articles. But she never exceeded her limit. She kept to the shilling per week and always made sure that she had reduced her bill sufficiently before getting further clothes that would still keep her within that weekly payment of a shilling. He had an affable relationship with my mother and would often stand and joke with her in our cramped kitchen. Then one day in a burst of friendly chatter she asked him did he give out Christmas presents? He gave her his address and told her to call with him on December 24th. There would be something waiting for her.

As we waited in his sitting room I was stupified with wonder at the soft carpeting on the floor, the shining furniture, the pictures on the walls and the warmth and richness pervading everything. My mother was quiet and shy and a little nervous. She had never sat in such luxury in her life, and frantically tried to flick away the little puddles of water that trickled from our clothes onto the carpet. Mr Peshkin came back to us with a paper-covered parcel and she thanked him for his kindness. He offered her the compliments of the season and showed us out into the night.

It was blowing and raining heavily now, and bitterly cold; and my mother found it difficult to hold on to her present and keep her shawl wrapped around her. The sucking noises from my shoes echoed down the deserted avenue and I trembled uncontrollably. When we reached the Antrim Road my mother said we would take a tram to Carlisle Circus which was close enough to home. We crossed the road to a request stop just in time to meet a clanking old red tram heading for the city centre. My mother gave the conductor her penny fare and a halfpenny for mine and sat clutching tightly to Mr Peshkin's gift. After we had been on the tram for several minutes she realised with a shock that it was going via Duncairn Gardens instead of Carlisle Circus. This would mean a long detour, but it was too late to do anything about it and so we sat there, miserable and cold, unwilling to think of the long walk home.

We reached home drenched and exhausted. My mother set her present on a chair and then hung her soaked shawl along the banister. I sat down numbly in front of the fire and gazed at the parcel. My hair was plastered over my face and steam rose up from my body. My mother's cheeks were drawn with tiredness and her long black hair was dangling damply over her shoulders, but her eyes held anticipation and with a smile she reached down to take the paper wrappings off the present. She pulled the paper away hurriedly for she was agog to know what it might be. She was little used to Christmas gifts, especially from outside the family circle. The paper fell away to reveal a tinny, brass-coloured ornamental pot, the kind made to hold a flowerpot. We both stared and stared. We wondered what it could be. It was lifted up and examined. We traced the thin filligree work with our fingers. Still mystified, my mother cleared a spot for it on the sideboard and sat down. She looked at it and she looked at me, and then she smiled and there were tears in her eyes. She put her arms around me and we both shook with laughter.

When Mr Peshkin called the following week for his shilling my mother went over to the sideboard and started to search for the payment book. The Jew, with the warmth of wisdom remarked, 'That old book is always hard to find.' Mother looked flushed, then with a little laugh she said, 'Dear me, I have it in the pot now. I put it there for handiness.' Out of the brassy pot she pulled all the key documents: insurance policies, the rent book, the grocery book from Cook on the Old Lodge Road, and finally the drapery tick book. Mr Peshkin drew deeply on his cigarette, then remarked, 'I knew you would like it. Everything has its use.'

I confess that I had a liking for the Jew. He was always pleasant and full of jokes. My father liked him too. Mr Peshkin would offer him a cigarette and they would yarn about the awful things that had occurred in Lithuania to so many of his race. I discovered that Mr Peshkin himself had been born in Carlisle Street on the Old Lodge Road but I was not mature enough to grasp the fullness of the tragedy that had befallen his people.

f the weather was not too good or the nights too cold Blackie and I would sneak into the Roseheath Dart Club in Downing Street. It was warm and comfortable, and the games held great drama for us... 'Quiet please... quiet please... Walt James to throw... thirteen, twenty-seven, sixty-seven the thrower.' With the lights dimmed and the men intent on their darts, we melted into the background, soaking up the atmosphere, and sitting on the edge of our benches as the final double was sought.

Blackie and I met Marie and Lizzie in Downing Street. Marie flitted round like a princess oblivious to our worship, although at times she was more approachable than sister Liz. They lived close to the Roseheath Dart Club, and we put up ropes for them on the lamp post outside their door on which they would swing, chatter and laugh. I especially welcomed these night-time cavortings, for the poor light of the old gaslamp helped to hide the patches in my clothes, allowing me to feel much more at ease.

We vied with one another for the privilege of helping the girls with their homework. The sisters would praise us for being so brainy and of course we liked them. Marie was always pleasant and kind, and Liz was more aloof, more haughty perhaps, but they were both goddesses, and so hair was combed, faces were scrubbed, teeth were washed and each of us would try to speak more genteely in their presence.

This little world of rapture crashed around us when the girls moved away to a better street. We came out of the darts room one night and the lamppost was without its rope and the beautiful ones were gone. The windows were bare of curtains. They had moved away that morning. We never went back to Roseheath, and never again heard Marie's happy laughter or looked upon the proud face of Liz. Both of us were miserable for almost two weeks, for we had lost Treasure Island and the Ben Gunns and Long John Silvers and our tents and two girls in pretty quick succession. Two weeks is a desperate long time in the eyes of little boys.

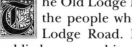he Old Lodge Road seldom received its full title from the people who knew it. It was simply known as the Lodge Road. It was crowded with little shops and public houses and it and the nearby Shankill Road supplied the simple requirements of the people of the Hammer.

Davison's bread shop especially appealed to me. I loved the smell of it and often stood at the window gazing entranced at the trays of cream buns, fruit loaves and sponge cakes. On the rare occasions when my mother could afford a slab of lemon cake, or Madeira Cake to give the proper name, it delighted me to be inside, surrounded by such appetising things, and marvelling at the shopgirl's dexterity as she wrapped up the precious piece in super thin brown tissue paper. One never threw this paper away. It was too valuable for polishing windows.

Next door to Davison's was a draper's shop. I was only inside it once. That was on the melancholy occasion of my mother's death. I would have been fourteen. My father was left to bring up the six of us on his own. He took me there for a black tie and a black armband to wear at my mother's funeral.

Gray's fruit and vegetable shop was further along, and although I often bought fourpence worth of soup vegetables for the Sunday dinner I never had an apple, a pear, or an orange out of Gray's.

The two shops that held the greatest fascination for me were the ones owned by Mr Lazarus and the Deitches. They were Jews of course, poor Jews, sharing in the general poverty of the area. But to me their shops were Aladdin's caves and I used to stand in the cold of a winter's night peering through the gaslit windows that protected so many joys. In Deitche's window a shepherd boy etched upon the tin side of a mouthorgan gave to me a dreamy wonder that it was me who was there. Myself on some Galilean hillside in the bright warmth of the sun and the blue skies and soft, sweet music. The cold is forgotten and in my imagination I am playing magic airs with such finesse that birds hush their song in adoration.

There was a silver fountain pen in Mr Lazarus's window, gleaming and important looking beside its fancy box. It could be had for ninepence and me wanting it, all the long winter days and nights of wanting. In time and in various ways, with a halfpenny here and a penny there, I eventually made my triumphal entrance and bought the pen from Mr Lazarus.

Mr Lazarus, nicknamed 'Wee Head,' had a tiny bald head and a heavy accent. He thanked me for the purchase and I could hardly wait to get home to fill it up from my father's Stephen's Ink bottle. But the pen leaked. I unscrewed it to find its rubber tube had rotted away. It had sat too long in the damp shop window. I tried hard to keep the tears from my eyes.

'You haf not used it vite,' squeaked Mr Lazarus. His wife came out into the shop. His son came out into the shop. They held their hands up in horror at the sight of the poor pen. 'Vat haf you done with it?'

The gaslamps were spluttering from the ceiling as the little pen was laid out on the counter, dripping from its mortal wounds.

'It can not be changed now,' cried Mrs Lazarus wringing her hands. 'You haf it ruined.' I was ruined also, but I had to keep it. It was a lesson to me. Maybe they just didn't believe me. Maybe my ninepence was a lifeline to them, to purchase a meal perhaps, for they had it hard too. Mr Lazarus hanged himself. He died in chronic poverty.

The Deitches lived next door. They were two girls: one plump, jolly and very dark, the other slim and fairish with sad brown eyes. They sold comics, magazines and newspapers, pipe tobacco, cigarettes, sweets, toys and potted herrings. There was always a stench of fish and olive oil from the fish barrel in the corner.

The plump one would sometimes call me to mind the shop whilst she was gone for two minutes on an errand. The errand was to the bookie's shop around the corner in Foreman Street to do thruppence each way, but when she came back she always gave me a back number of *Funny Wonder.* Like Lazarus they were poor, but years afterwards they were to fare better in a confectionery shop they somehow managed to obtain on the Antrim Road. Maybe the plump one had at long last broken the bookie.

t the Boundary Street end of the Shankill Road there was a public house which had its interior decorated with all kinds of stuffed animal heads. On a damp afternoon I was walking past the pub when I saw a crowd of men hammering at a door across the street. A woman was shouting down to the mob from an upstairs window. 'Will you go away for he's not in the house!'

I stopped to view the commotion and just then a man jumped off an approaching tram and turned into the street. As soon as he entered it the mob let out a roar and made for the man, who dashed back onto the Shankill Road. And then he slipped in the wet street and fell heavily, and the shouting, ranting crowd tore into him with their boots, and kicked him without mercy. Kicked him and kicked him until the man was a bleeding, torn, unrecognisable piece of humanity. Then they ran away and the woman who had been at the upstairs window was lying across the bloody form, screaming and calling, 'Oh my God, oh my God!' Two policemen came running up the street with batons in one hand and revolvers in the other, and another crowd gathered in the rain. The police ordered them to be on their way but the woman was still screaming and the rain lashing down, making the blood flow off along the gutter. I stood stock still, unable to move. Now a constable was shouting at the woman, who was covered in blood, to shut up, and when the other policeman came across to me I still couldn't move so he kicked me.

I asked my father a multitude of questions but I was told to stay away from the Shankill if I didn't want to be killed. I think the dead man was a catholic. The couple had been mixed.

So I stayed around my little street playing marbles and relievo, and was in bed before dark. Then later in the stillness sometimes shots could be heard. Police tenders rumbled heavily down the cobbled street making the walls of the house vibrate. Wooden shutters enclosed the windows of our house and we had two bolts and a heavy lock on the front door. The atmosphere in the bedroom would be stifling and I used to dream about the man who had been kicked to death, a dream that did not quickly go away.

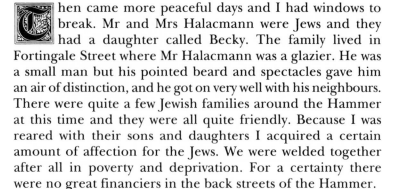hen came more peaceful days and I had windows to break. Mr and Mrs Halacmann were Jews and they had a daughter called Becky. The family lived in Fortingale Street where Mr Halacmann was a glazier. He was a small man but his pointed beard and spectacles gave him an air of distinction, and he got on very well with his neighbours. There were quite a few Jewish families around the Hammer at this time and they were all quite friendly. Because I was reared with their sons and daughters I acquired a certain amount of affection for the Jews. We were welded together after all in poverty and deprivation. For a certainty there were no great financiers in the back streets of the Hammer.

I was guilty of smashing quite a few windows in the middle class milieu around Eglington Street and Cliftonpark Avenue, and of passing this information to Mr Halacmann, who would reward me on a sliding scale if he were engaged to replace them. Parlour windows were worth a penny, scullery windows one halfpenny; but a decorative pane in a front door won me the magnificent sum of fourpence. Mr Halacmann walked around with heavy panes of glass slung in a frame across his shoulders, and a pot of putty and knives, and he would call on spec at doors. The business of breaking windows didn't trouble my conscience too much, for the folk in Cliftonpark Avenue were doctors and solicitors who had flashy cars, maids and housekeepers.

Mrs Halacmann was a well educated woman who spoke a couple of languages fluently, and who also made the most wonderful suits and dresses out of bits and pieces of discarded cloth. She was knocked down one day on the Lodge Road and killed instantly. Her husband never got over the shock and he too was gone six weeks later. And so Becky was left alone, a dumpty piece of a girl with no great looks and little brainpower.

The synagogue helped her with food and money and for a long time she was engaged in a most bizarre job. Old Jews who had no known relatives and who had died in lodgings or homes, or whatever, finished up in Becky's house in a wooden case in her backyard until the day came for their burial. These times were bad times, times of misery, debt, despair and early deaths. Tuberculosis and rickets were rife amongst this almost forgotten people, for they were ignored and left to rot by church and state.

I had no real feelings then of rebellion against the lot of the poor; I was still a boy. I was far too young to fix reasons or notions to the circumstances that made for one-room slums, stricken mothers, and meals concocted from pieces of fatty meat scraps. I had an innate sense of being respectful to wealth and authority, and of course many kids had little option but to respect rich masters however foul those masters might be. There were times when one just had to grovel.

What I did possess was a zany sense of humour, and I chuckled with laughter at the idea of spiders being lifted from rags to riches when I placed them inside open windows belonging to the houses of the affluent.

There were times too when our gang would return from a day spent at Greencastle looking for willicks. Bags of crabs would be pushed through letter boxes in comfortable Eglington Street. I would be doubled up with guffs of laughter when I pictured some solicitor trying to explain to the health inspectors that his house was being overrun with crabs... 'If you live at the seaside, sir, you may be outside our authority...'

'Damn it man I live in Eglington Street off the Old Lodge Road!'

And though I played many pranks upon middleclass Jews I would also do little jobs for them, such as lighting their fires on a Saturday, which is their Sabbath. I was sorry when increasing unrest forced them to move. Situated betwixt Orange and Green they became more and more the object of mindless bigotry and violence. The grand houses soon fell into slums as the money necessary for their upkeep disappeared.

ne great distinction the Hammer possessed was the fact that it had what was judged to be the smallest street in Belfast. This was Knoxs Street, that ran its few yards from Leadbetter Street to Foreman Street, emerging from underneath the bedroom of one of the houses in Foreman Street. All that was in Knoxs Street were two gateways belonging to coalmen – Campbell and Lockington – and the side door of the *Busy Bee* public house. These features overcrowded the little street.

I and my pals were a bit wary of using the entry during the hours of darkness, for the gloom was barely dispersed by the old gaslamp perched high on a wall bracket. When you walked or ran through it, echoes filled your ears, and the drumming feet would sound like the hooves of ghostly horses.

The place held a kind of fascination for me, for Rutherford Street to which I had now moved, directly faced it. Part of that fascination lay in the sounds and smells emanating from the *Busy Bee*, which helped to chase away the banshees and demons that flitted about it. Sometimes when courage was strong upon me I would stand beside the steamy door and listen to the voices.

There was the high distinct voice of Mr Sproule the sign writer: 'The Jews are God's chosen people.' There was the harsh voice of oul' Jimmy White arguing about football – Irish football. There was the quavering voice of Jack McKeown who was our next door neighbour, ordering his dog to sup up its porter and lie down, and the pugnacious voice of Mr Fleming: 'The willicks from Greencastle are the best in the country. I don't give a damn what anybody says about sewage!'

There was laughter and babbles and groans and coughs and clearing of throats and the odd wild shouts of 'I'm yer man. Outside and I'll bate the bloody head off ye!' And often in the uncertain light of the gaslamp two figures would reel out stripped to the waist and stand toe to toe, walloping and banging each other until blood blinded, or exhaustion overcame them.

And I stood there, wide-eyed and a little frightened, shuddering each time a fist pounded a crimson face; stood amongst a circle of tipsy spectators in the narrow confines of the street, and they urging on the fighters and Jack's dog howling to the dark sky because he is as drunk as the rest.

I did manage to get into the *Busy Bee* one afternoon when things were not so boisterous. There had been a death in one of the nearby streets a few days before, and I went round to the bin to see if there were any empty stout bottles put there after the wake. This hardly ever occurred for bottles were charged for and had to be returned to the public houses in order to get one's money back. However this day I was in luck and managed to retrieve about three dozen bottles. I brought them home and washed the labels off carefully, for the supplier's name was not the same as delivered to the *Busy Bee*. I got a halfpenny for each of the bottles, and my father was grateful for the one and thruppence I was able to give him, and a sumptuous meal was had by all that afternoon.

As usual on that sun-kissed day in summer Tommy Irvine was sitting in the shaded bar with his bottle of stout beside the ever present draughts board. He was an expert at the game and was familiar with a bewildering variety of openings like the 'Ayrshire Lassie,' 'Will-O-The-Wisp,' 'Laird And Lady,' and many others. So good was he, for he was unbeaten in the pub, that games against anyone brave enough to take him on, were almost his sole source of obtaining drink.

Years of competing around working mens' clubs such as the one in Danube Street and in bars had given to Tommy in his healthy old age the finesse of the professional, the polish of the true artist, always ready with the proper defence against innumerable variations from those willing to bet a stout hoping to beat the foxy old codger.

Then big Walter Simpkins lumbered in. He was a giant of a man, a house repairer by trade and he was still a bit of a stranger in the district, having only arrived on the Old Lodge Road about two months previously. He could usually be seen in the pub at weekends, his head buried in some newspaper oblivious to all the crack, and an old briar pipe stuck in his mouth. He called for a pint of porter and sat down near to Tommy.

'A warm day,' said he to Tommy.

'Ay, it's a brave warm day indeed mister, and good to see it.'

'You're a draughts player,' said Simpkins. 'Anyhow whenever I come in you seem to be always playing.'

'Well now ye might say that and other folk might say different. Do ye play yourself?'

'It's a good while since I played the game. I just play the odd time in the house by myself mostly.'

'Oh, ye play by the book then?'

'I do. I do indeed.'

'Would ye fancy a bit of a game while ye're in? Best out of three for a bottle?'

'I wouldn't mind at all,' said Simpkins, 'for it will be good to get away from yon chandering woman of mine for a while.'

I heard most of this conversation as I partially concealed myself behind one of the four little cubicles in the bar – boxes they were usually called – which gave a modicum of privacy to the brave woman who would slip in for a drink. I was in a bold mood that day, for the only other times I had seen inside the place were whenever the side door was left ajar to allow the fumes of tobacco to filter out, and I would take a hasty glance inside and look around at the different characters. I liked the game and used to play at home with my father. I always beat him for I used to watch the games played in the bandstand in Woodvale Park, and I had picked up some of the moves.

Tommy answered the man in a ruminative tone. 'Do ye know,' he said, 'there's nothing as bad as a chandering woman. The way they go on could drive ye around the bend.'

The big man got up and collected his pint, then sat himself down facing the old expert.

'Och now she's not that bad. You see, she used to be a doffing mistress in Linfield Spinning Mill. She retired with the oul' pains a while back, but she still thinks she has that whistle on her apron that she used to call up the doffers.'

'You're not too long around here?' queried Tommy.

'Ah, no,' said Simpkins. 'We came from the Sandy Row direction because the house here has a bigger yard to keep my ladders in.'

'My name's Tommy Irvine.' ventured the old man.

'You can call me Walter Simpkins.'

'Well Walter, we'll toss for who goes first.'

'Not at all. Away you go.'

I was about to leave when I noticed a little knot of spectators gathering around the two men, so I melted in with them.

'Would ye fancy a bit of a game while ye're in?
Best out of three for a bottle?'

Tommy set up the men on the board with the black next to himself. He opened with the 'Fife,' probably the most interesting opening in the game. Then he gave a low whistle, for Simpkins countered with the 'Defiance.' This would prevent the formation of the 'Fife'. Yes, there it was – 27 to 23, and unless it was a random move, this man had to be watched, so Tommy gulped down some of his stout and made his move 8 to 11. Of course most of the manoeuvres on the board were Greek to me but the atmosphere was thrilling. And no one thought to throw me out. I was standing with the men in the *Busy Bee*.

The game became intriguing, and this was not lost on the spectators, quite a few of whom were knowledgeable about draughts, and indeed the odd bet was wagered on the outcome of the game. Simpkins was a grand player.

After a while the watching throng sensed that the unbeaten Tommy Irvine was in trouble. The old fellow was coming down on the stout too often and there was a hush in the bar that spelt out a lot of sympathy for him. So this first game went to Simpkins, with a consequent scribbling in a tiny notebook by the man taking the bets.

However Tommy won the second game, and now it all depended upon this third and last game. Just then the front door of the pub was flung back almost off its hinges. Standing in the entrance was a tiny flinty faced woman, red hair brought round to the back of her head in a tight bun. She glanced at the crowd for a few moments and then in cutting tones spoke out. 'Is there a big lump of a Walter Simpkins in here?'

'Quiet woman!' someone shouted back.

'No, I'll not be quiet,' retorted the little woman. 'I'm his wife and I'm looking for him.'

Simpkins had been so intent upon the board that he didn't realise his wife was calling at the open door. Then when her voice shrilled more loudly he heard her, and with his concentration broken, made the fatal move, 30 to 25. This would lose the game for him for a certainty and old Tommy chuckled to himself. He was happy now.

Walter Simpkins stood up and glared across at his diminutive wife, 'Well woman, want do you want, traipsing after me to a pub?'

'You walked up here when you knew quite well I was to go out with you to the shops.'

'Let it wait then until I finish my game.'

'I want you down home now,' insisted the woman,

'I'll be down inside ten minutes,' growled the big man.

Some of the company then spoke up. 'Let the man finish his game missus.'

She left; but the game was over. Old Tommy was still the *Busy Bee* champion.

'Boys a boys ye were near yourself there, Tommy,' one of the happy punters said after Simpkins had gone.

'Sooner or later they always make the wrong move,' smiled the old man, pulling a bottle close to him.

'I never saw thon sort of move in the 'Fife' anyway.'

'A new move son, a new move. And it might as well be called the 'Chandering Woman.'

nother interesting part of Knoxs Street was Mr Lockington's gateway. Through it I watched Mr Lockington's father darning coal sacks with a big needle and a ball of twine, the horse stabled in the yard behind him. Everything being so small it was always a job to manoeuvre it and the cart in and out. Everything was tricky, so much so that when old Mrs Lockington died they had to lower her coffin from an upstairs window, as the stairs were too narrow.

Coming through the entry one day I saw Lockington's gate wide open, and a gathering of people inside. Jack McKeown was there with his dog, and so was my big brother Sam, with his dog. I stopped to ask what was going on. I soon found out. Old Mr Lockington was working at a huge pile of empty coal sacks and as he began to separate them he shouted, 'Get ready!' Then out they came, dozens and dozens of frantic, leaping mice. In the dogs went for a not-so-merry-go-round of yelping, snapping, darting savagery with no quarter given: slavering, biting jaws, and the mice dashing up walls then falling back into gaping mouths; and everything a-whirling and a-scurrying until the sounds became less and the ground was littered with little corpses. The dogs panted, the spectators panted, and I felt grieved and helpless. I had always been fond of mice. I had fed them and trained them to promenade. But the men didn't see what they had done as cruelty. There was nothing I could do.

 was going to school a few weeks later and going via Knoxs Street. I was looking swell, feeling dandy, wearing what had lately been my Sunday suit. Great to get rid of the old jersey and patched trousers. Hair combed and boots shining, I could have jumped over the moon. I didn't jump over the moon but out of sheer exuberance took a jump across a pile of sludge from a blocked drain, miscalculated its extent and pitched myself headlong into the slimy putrifaction. I dragged myself up in horror. Tears filled my eyes when I saw the state of my clothes. I dripped from head to foot.

Young Mr Lockington's wife spotted my awful condition and called me over. She procured basins of cold water and brushes and did a wonderful job of cleaning me up. I was overwhelmed by her kindness and tears weren't too far away. She made me stand in front of the fire whilst I was sponged down and wiped clean.

Although I endured the long day at school with a trace of stickiness and the suspicion of an odour, none came to know about my fateful leap into Knoxs Street. But that little street gave me a wonderful education. Where else would I have learnt about ghosts, Jewish emigration, the long jump, bare knuckle fighting and blood sports?

5

 was making my way towards a papershop in Agnes Street to buy half a dozen canes for Mr Smyth, my teacher. Of late several canes had been cunningly nicked by a razor blade, and when Greenlees, Garret or Hawthorne stood up for their almost daily whacks the cane would split on impact with their defiant outstretched palms. Mr Smyth used to hide his canes on top of a large cupboard up in the gallery – the part of the classroom where the desks were raised up in tiers like a miniature football stand. However I had found this hiding place and the mutilations had continued, for as well as being the trusted fetcher of the canes, I was also the phantom nicker.

As I came around by Wellwyne Street a large lorry and trailer rattled past me on its solid tyres. Just then a child ran straight between them. Its distracted mother flung herself after it, and was dragged by the towing mechanism for some yards before the lorry stopped with grindings and clankings. There was blood on the roadway, and a crowd screaming and shouting. I was pushed against the gable wall of a house, stupified with shock. The woman lying there all dirty and bleeding was crying loudly and calling, 'My baby, my baby,' and an old lady in a shawl was wiping the dirt and blood off the child's head and I walked off in a kind of daze to the shop.

When I came out with the canes I couldn't face going back to the terrible scene but walked back via Ariel Street. I returned with the canes, in a sort of awful stupor. Mr Smyth got me to sit down, and asked why I was so white looking. The incident

shook me. But in a strange way it also taught me which side of
the law I wanted to be on. From that day on there was no
more razoring of canes.

own in Rumford Street there was a dispensary office.
This was where you could obtain a free doctor and
medicine, depending on your means. Inside you faced
a glass fronted partition, on the other side of which was an
inquisitorial clerk. 'What's the full name of the sick person?'
he would commence. 'Address... Age... Total Income... Rent?'
And finally, 'What's wrong with them?'

Later in the day Dr Osborne would arrive, and puff and
blow his way up our narrow stairs. He was a short roly-poly
man with a huge walrus moustache, and he hated visiting the
kitchen houses. 'Damn rabbit warrens,' he would fume as he
squeezed himself up the narrow stairway. Then on his way
down he would snort: 'If you people opened your bowels
more often there would be a lot less sickness.' Then he would
scribble out a prescription. It was nearly always the same kind
of medicine. A pink concoction for the 'flu and feverish
colds, a dark evil smelling liquid for cramps and various
other complaints. The patients were so scared of him they
would keep the unused medicine for months on end, long
after it was useful, in fact it had probably changed into another
chemical, rather than have him re-visit.

n Rumford Street there was also a bacon curing factory,
which in later years was to become a Coca-Cola depot.
I loved the smell of the salted bacon and so did the
bluebottles and cats. And so apparently did the winos, for
quite often its front gates would be littered with empty bottles.
When I got out of school one day a lot of people were making
their way towards Rumford Street and the talk was 'Houdini's
here. He's going to pull a tram up the Shankill by his teeth!'

Actually he was at the Shankill Road end of Craven Street,
just at the bottom of Rumford Street, and he didn't look
much like a Houdini for he was rather scrawny and pasty
looking. He was just getting up from a bed of nails and his
back looked like a piece of streaky bacon from the nearby

factory. I was with Blackie and Wossie Hamilton, and we pushed through the crowd to the front. 'Houdini' took a rope from out of an old bag and challenged anyone in the audience to tie him up. He said he could free himself from any kind of knots. Oul' Jimmy Brown came forward, chewing away as usual on his plug of Warhorse tobacco. 'Bejasus young fellow, I'll tie ye up alright. Ye're talking to an ex-navyman ye know.'

He tied him up indeed! The rope was around his neck, around his legs, around his arms; up, in, out and over; knotted here, knotted there; sheep shanks and half-hitches and oul' Jimmy puffing and blowing and spitting out tobacco, and Joe Watson starting to sing, 'Tie him to the yard-arm till he's sober.' Eventually poor old 'Houdini' was wound up like a spool filled with thread, and then the escape commenced. Wriggle, wriggle, wriggle. Stand on one leg, then on the other; breathe in, breathe out. Then shake, wriggle, and in one minute he was free of the rope. 'Bejasus,' said oul' Jimmy. 'Ye wouldn't have done that on me a wheen a' years back.' Somebody shouted, 'Good job you're not the hangman Jimmy.'

Then 'Houdini', sweating profusely, picked up a whip with a very long lash. He asked for a lady volunteer to come forward and he would knock a cigarette from her lips with his whip. There was a bit of laughing and good natured banter, then a girl called Dolly Stirling sauntered towards him. Dolly no doubt imagined this was her chance to break into the new-fangled talkies, for she had great ideas. 'Houdini' told her there was nothing to be afraid of and that she was very beautiful. Then he stuck a Woodbine in her mouth. She stood there looking like Pearl White and the crowd went quiet. The whip cracked and sped out like a striking snake. And it did strike! It struck her on the ear and the blood spurted and she gave a scream and Mrs Bell shouted, 'He's killed her!'

But she wasn't killed, and after 'Houdini' had cleaned up her ear, he gave her threepence. Then he packed up his equipment and walked up the Shankill Road, still with his shirt off, and his back still showing the marks of the nails, and

Watson shouting after him, 'Ye ought to be tied up!'

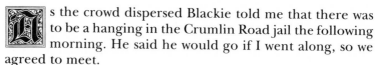s the crowd dispersed Blackie told me that there was to be a hanging in the Crumlin Road jail the following morning. He said he would go if I went along, so we agreed to meet.

As we crossed over the waste ground at Fortingale Street the next morning and made our way up Florence Place to the Crumlin Road we felt very excited at joining the crowds who were heading for the jail. It was a fine sunny morning, and a horse drawn watercart was wending its way down the Old Lodge Road 'laying the dust' from its squirting rear pipe. It seemed as if half of Belfast had turned up, and a stranger could be forgiven for imagining he was about to witness a public execution.

'There's somebody waving from a window,' shouted a woman to the crowd, and all eyes searched for the window. 'Where, where, missus? It'll be your man,' called out someone, and there was a buzz of chatter... 'Do you think he'll get a last minute reprieve...?' 'They should hang all murderers...' 'Oh no, I don't believe in hanging...'

Then a small group of people began to sing 'Abide With Me' and the chatter and the loud talk eased to a silence, and then, like the first gradualness of an incoming tide the whole crowd gave voice, and the blending voices rose like a prayer. As the last lines of the great hymn flowed forth a tiny door in the large gate opened and an officer fastened a sheet upon the door. The man had been executed, and young as I was I felt myself tremble with unexplained indignation. I saw a few tears in Blackie's eyes and in the eyes of others, and there was a great hush like the two minute's silence. Then I turned and in my bare feet walked towards the school, soon to be caught up once again in the great swell of living in the Hammer.

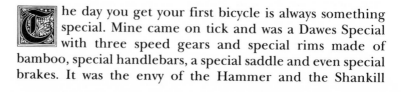he day you get your first bicycle is always something special. Mine came on tick and was a Dawes Special with three speed gears and special rims made of bamboo, special handlebars, a special saddle and even special brakes. It was the envy of the Hammer and the Shankill

Road, for then as now most of the children were bicycle mad.

Before I was lucky enough to get my racing machine most of my spare pennies were spent on hiring out an old second-hand bike – a penny for fifteen minutes. There was a man who hired these in Matier Street, and to keep his hiring list in order he gave all his bicycles a name. I used to stand in the man's yard and read down that list as if they were the details of ocean liners out on high and mystic seas. Names like Titanic, Bermuda, Adventurer, Golden Wave, Silver Streak and Little Prince. Beside the names was a carefully ruled column giving the time the bicycle was hired out and when it was due back.

One day I was riding Little Prince. On this machine there were no special gears, no special wheels and no special brakes. Indeed there were no brakes at all, the sole of one's boot against the front tyre stopped her. It was pouring with rain and just as I was thinking of returning the bicycle at its expiry time a fire engine roared past, its clanging bell making the carthorses dance and jump.

It was a great fire. The stables belonging to a bakery on the Springfield Road were blazing and men were bringing out frightened horses from the building. Although it was lashing down the flames were erupting mountain high and as the smoke fanned out the road became almost invisible. It was my first sight of a large building on fire and I was goggle-eyed with excitement. What a tale this would be for the boys on Blenheim School steps!

Returning down the Shankill I got a puncture, but I was still able to steer Little Prince over its slippery square setts, as the granite road blocks were called. At the corner of Matier Street I met the usual gathering of youngsters begging to be allowed to bring back a bicycle in order to obtain the free ride. The owner didn't pay much attention to this practice for it was times, and not names, that were recorded on the hire sheet. I was an hour overdue, and I'm ashamed to say I got off and left the bike to them without the slightest twinge of conscience.

nyone who has visited Woodvale Park will know that its main entrance is in line with a very fast and tricky corner out there on the Woodvale Road. I got to know it very well on the day of the motorcycle races.

I had been up watching Stanley Woods scorching along doing about eighty miles an hour on his machine. Others said he went faster. Eighty miles an hour was it, I maintained. Nobody or nothing could go faster. After all I had some experience of miles per hour. My gang used to reckon that from Northumberland Street to the bad bend at Woodvale Park and back again was a mile. Blackie and I had run that distance in our bare feet many a Saturday afternoon. Before he got his watch with a picture of a train on the dial, Watson would time us from the clock that hung above the bakery near Northumberland Street. One Saturday I came tearing back to Northumberland Street from my run. Watson looked up at the clock then turned to me with emotion choking his voice. 'Jasus John, if you had been another two minutes quicker you would have been as good as the British champion.'

'I could have done it,' I gasped modestly, 'only I fell over a bin outside the Shankill library.'

Anyway, this day I got away from the motorbike race pretty fast with the aid of my great bicycle. Coming down the Ardoyne Road the wind shrieked past me and the tyres hummed on the bone dry road. I was certain people were looking after me with envy. I was sure that at times I was moving as fast as the motorcycles I had just finished watching.

The speed of my Dawes Special had now overcome the thrust of my legs and I felt supremely happy. If only I had had someone to time this stupendous effort... I slowed slightly as I whizzed past the junction of the Crumlin and the Woodvale Roads, then zeroed in on Woodvale corner. I clamped my rear brakes on to take the bend. Then nothing. The cable snapped. I was filled with terror. I took the corner in a wide sweep, rounding it safely but too fast to use the front brake. I seemed to pass into a haze as I careered ever onwards. Then a fellow cyclist came across me from a side street and I frantically altered course a fraction. But that fraction was too much and I went up the pavement with a sickening crunch of

wood and clanging of metal. Still clinging to the bicycle I
sailed through the open doors of a pub at the corner of
Cambrai Street to crash against the bar counter.

Amazingly, I had only skinned my knees and knuckles. But
the Dawes Special had a buckled front wheel, and a broken
cable and chain. I was made to sit down. An old fellow
insisted he was going to sing and raise a collection towards
the mending of the bike. So I sat with the hard drinkers
sipping a glass of lemonade and weeping, and the man sang
his song:

> *I dread the day you'll forget me Marguerite*
> *But oh I know it soon will come.*

Thunderous applause followed, and over four shillings was
raised towards the repair of my lovely machine. This was a
goodly sum although it would probably be fair to say it was
hardly raised because the audience appreciated the croakings
of the game old singer.

or some time afterwards I was a bit timorous of going
round that bend on a bike. Now and again I would
dismount making the excuse to Blackie that I was
thirsty and wanted a drink from the fountain which stood
inside the park. A metal cup hung from a chain and hot and
sticky kids usually swarmed round this bubbling geyser to
slake their thirsts. Blackie was doubtful about the cup:

'I tell you, it'll give you TB.'

'No it won't. Not if you spit the first drink out.'

There were grand houses hugging the bad corner opposite
the park. They had great hedges and fine gardens, and judging
by the pots on the chimneys each must have had quite a few
rooms. In the garden of one of the houses, in all their glory,
sat two marble statues. They were renowned in the district.
Probably they were poor copies of statues of Venus and Adonis,
but we all thought they were great. I mentioned them one
time to my headmaster, who smiled at his assistant. 'Ah Miss
Dickey, John is speaking of the Woodvale Marbles,' he said,
punning on the Elgin Marbles. Miss Dickey registered a

blank expression, and no doubt so did I, for I had no idea then of the wonderful statues that had adorned the frieze of the Parthenon in Greece. How could an urchin possibly know?

he park was bounded on its north side by Ballygomartin Brickworks and the dams; beyond that was the Forth River. Our idea of contentment was to fish there for the sticklebacks and the newts, which we knew as spricks and lizards.

Blackie maintained that the spricks were hatched from the dead dogs whose skeletons could be seen shining in the water. He warned us:

'Don't go into the water in your bare feet or the bloodsuckers will bleed you to death.'

'How do you know?'

'How do you think the dogs got dead? And what about the man's body found here one time, eh?'

'What about it?'

'It had no blood in it.'

We chased after the redbreasts or male sticklebacks, not knowing then that during the breeding season the male was adorned with a red breast to attract the female. And it was just splendid to tramp down the Woodvale Road past the Woodvale Marbles with all eyes on our jam jars filled with fiery monsters; and of course the little piece of weed for them to hide behind when it was sunny.

'Are they goldfish, wee fella?'

We never bothered to answer silly questions.

The Forth River was a great place. At least it was in those days before it got polluted by works' chemicals. Blackie led the outdoor sports and pastimes carried on along its length; the fishing, the running, the leap-frog, and the standing on your hands. He dared us to jump across the Forth at one of its widest points, and me and Gouldie, Watters and Young watched him clear it in one tremendous leap. Blackie was my hero as well as my friend. We were very brave and followed him, but our tremendous leaps only landed us in the water.

Young Sproule sometimes went with us to fish for the

lizards. His da was an important man who went to work wearing a collar and tie. He was a professional sign writer and painter and many a time I watched him standing on a ladder outside some shop on the Lodge Road painting ever so easily words like JAMES JOHNSTON HIGH CLASS BUTCHER. He was also very fond of porter, it killed the lead inhaled from the paint according to him. This was something that I would puzzle over because I knew the porter went into his stomach and not into his lungs.

One day Mr Sproule came staggering along on his way home as my father and I were standing at our door. Mr Sproule stopped and took a deep breath. 'Hi there Sammie. My missus was up yapping in the pub for me to come home. Did you notice her going past?'

'Ay, some minutes ago and she looked to be in a bad temper.'

'Sammie, I'm going to teach her a lesson. Bejasus I am.'

'What are you going to do?'

'Sammie, I'm going in and I'm going to pee on the floor.'

I put him on a par with a king after hearing this threat.

Enough of your impertinence woman! Stand aside whilst I pee upon thine carpet!

His son, who was called Robert, was tormented by his grannie. She had some kind of fixation about Robert ending up along with the lizards on the bottom of the Forth. If he were away at the fishing for more than two hours she was sure to be seen advancing over the clay hills yelling like some demented creature: 'Rabb-ee, Rabb-ee!'

Grannie Sproule was a thin person with long straggling red hair, and it was whispered by adults that she used her son's turpentine to oil her hair. She always wore a red flannel petticoat even on the warmest days of summer. And her walk! How the woman could walk! She had a rolling gait somewhat after the fashion of the marathon walkers, and with her feet encased in bedroom slippers she would roll up and down the Shankill Road, her hips knocking the stuffing out of each other, hair flying loose and arms flailing. Didn't give two hoots about other walkers.

'Hey missus, mind my child. You nearly knocked her kicking.'

'Go on ye ignorant oul' cat!'

When she would reach the top of a bank bordering her grandson's section of the river she would rattle off a volley of words at poor Robert, and even the lizards would hide quivering under the stones. Everyone was scared of her, and when she was in full flight she barely paused for breath.

'If I come down there I'll throw you into the bloody water you and your stinking fish and your trousers soaking and I don't know what you see in this crowd of rubbish you're with...'

> *Queenie queenie Caroline*
> *Dipped her hair in turpentine.*
> *Turpentine to make it shine,*
> *Queenie queenie Caroline.*

And then when the fishing had ended we would have a dare as we walked back through the park. The green verges were filled with flowers, all pinks and yellows and blues and reds. Marigolds, love-in-the-mist, roses and daisies and clarkia. I liked the flowers and their orderliness and the scent and the buzzing of the honey bees and the erratic flights of the butterflies.

> *Where flowers are, God is,*
> *And I am free.*

But the banks were also planted with signs: *Keep off the verge. Penalty for pulling flowers £5.* Nervously we would look round for the ranger, a man to be reckoned with, and if there was no sight of him, jump on the verge and jump off just as quickly and run like blazes. And oh God, the spricks spilling out on the path and Blackie with a bit of glass in his foot and he running like someone with one leg shorter than the other and wondering too if he has lost a redbreast... And no flowers touched, not one.

onsidering conditions in the Shankill and the Hammer, with mixed families often sleeping in one room, the realities of sex were slow to intrude upon otherwise quick and active minds. For instance, we were completely baffled by the trio of men who used to emerge furtively from the bushes beside the banks of the Forth equipped with telescopes. Blackie imagined they were birdwatchers. Gouldie said they could be bosses watching for men slacking in the nearby brickfields. I suggested that they might be spying on courting couples.

'What would they be watching them for?'

'To see them kissing.'

'God that's daft; coming away up here to see somebody having a kiss!'

What of course we didn't realise then was that they were voyeurs, known better then in Belfast by the term squatters, and not to be confused with persons who took possession of houses illegally. The men absolutely ignored us, probably because we were just kids, and whilst we hunted and fished for spricks and lizards they indulged in their viewing for what must have been a couple of hours.

One day a few of us were making our way up the Shankill with our jars and nets. It was a hot day and of course all of us were in our bare feet and ready for a good day's sport. In front of us was a man we did not know in company with a young woman we did know. She lived close to the Hammer and had the reputation of being a 'bad woman,' which meant to us that she drank in pubs with different men. However we paid scant attention to the couple and they soon faded from our minds when they disappeared into the tall grass.

Sometime later there was a commotion in the bushes near to us and we saw this trio with their telescopes. One of the men was excited, calling out to his mates, 'Jasus will you look at that, she's stripping off!' I looked at Watters and Watters looked at me, then Blackie said, 'Come on, let's crawl up through the grass and see what's going on.' We did just that, getting down like Indian braves and crawling in the direction of the bushes the spyglass man had in view. And what a shock we got when we reached the bushes for there was the man on top of the bad woman who, to cap it all, was naked.

Our eyes were popping out at the sight, but before we recovered our senses Gouldie had picked up an old dandelion root and flung it at the man's bare backside. He jerked up like a startled rabbit and the woman gave a scream so we scurried back to our jars like greased lightning. One of the spyglass men was waiting for us and he was looking very angry. He picked up our jars containing the redbreasts and the lizards and flung them into the river. 'Now buzz off,' he snarled at us, 'and don't come back.'

There was a great discussion that night about the naked man and woman. Naturally we sensed something wasn't right as she was a bad woman. Watters said they were probably sun bathing. Gouldie said it was a funny way to sunbathe. Blackie said the man must have really loved the bad woman to be kissing her with no clothes on.

I said I would ask my da about it.

'I thought you were up there to catch spricks?'

'But these men were watching them as well...'

'Just stay away from that Forth River. I'm telling you now.'

'But why did they have no clothes on?'

'She's a bad bitch, that's why, so no more fishing up there.'

ith the Forth out of bounds we decided to visit the museum. We had often discussed going there but for some reason or other had never ventured to the south end of the city. Now we had made up our minds to see the mummy woman.

The attendant looked us over with evident distaste, noting particularly that none of us had footwear.

'Where do you think you kids are going?'

'To see the mummy woman, mister.'

'I see,' said he, pushing out a chest decorated with war ribbons and rubbing his chin. 'Well, in you go, but no mischief now or I'll have you all prosecuted.'

And so we padded along the chill terrazzo floor looking around in awe at the great treasures. Then we met the mummy woman.

'God, John, she's not very old.'

'Don't talk so loudly, Blackie; show respect for the dead.'

'She's really in Heaven though, isn't she?'

Our motley little band, ragged and unshod, walked around

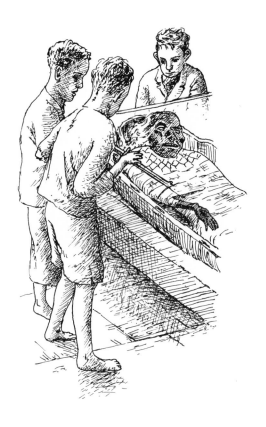

'Where do you think you kids are going?'
'To see the mummy woman, mister.'

the wonderland in an attitude akin to reverence.

Happy without radios or gramophones; unaware of the political seduction that assisted in keeping us in poverty, and knowing nothing of the sophisticated aloofness of the more affluent visitors, we left the museum that day with cold feet and glowing minds, and every wonderful item in the building safe and secure.

The attendant was at the exit door and our chatter seemed to infect him with a greater measure of friendliness.

'Did you see the mummy woman, then, you kids?'

'Ay, mister, and she's not a woman. She's a girl.'

'Did she scare you?'

'Girls don't scare us, mister.'

T hen there came a time when I was to meet a man with one leg, a man with one hand, a man with a patch over one eye, and a man who could speak a little French. They were in the habit of standing at the Lodge Road end of Boundary Street and quite often I would stand there with them, hypnotised by their gossip.

The man with one leg asked, 'How long is a piece of string?'

The man with the patch over one eye said, 'What thickness would the string be?'

'It doesn't matter what thickness it is.'

The man with one hand said it did matter, for over a certain thickness the string would have to be called a rope.

One-leg said let it be a bloody rope.

The man who could speak a little French said one could often be misled over words.

One-leg said it didn't matter a damn whether it was string, rope or sausages; so, how long was anything?

Eyepatch said that when the Indian Rope Trick was being performed no one could really estimate the rope's length because so much of it was up in the air with a boy climbing up to nowhere and the other end was coiled up on the ground.

One-leg asked me for God's sake to get him a piece of string, and when I obliged him, he held it tightly in one hand and said to the others, 'How long is it?'

All admitted they didn't know and One-leg said, 'I'll put you out of your misery, for it's twice half its length.'

Eyepatch said, give some people enough rope and they would hang themselves.

The Linguist wished to know if those people included politicians? One-hand said he wasn't at all sure if capital punishment should be allowed save in exceptional circumstances. One-leg said he wasn't scared of being the hangman if he were allowed to hang up all the exceptional cases sitting behind big desks in the City Hall.

Then commenced an argument about a problem met by carters on their rounds. 'The fact of the matter is,' said One-leg, 'people have to have provisions made for them by any sensible government.'

'I doubt if it is possible to find a sensible government,' remarked Eyepatch.

'That may be,' said One-leg, 'but the fact is that a carter is allowed by law to relieve himself against the nearside wheel of his cart.'

'The law is not the government,' said the Linguist, 'always remember that.'

One-leg asked for my opinion and I remembered a piece out of Dickens and said the law was an ass.

One-hand said that an ass was an intelligent animal and worthy of respect.

Eyepatch remarked that he had experience with donkeys in foreign lands and that sometimes they acted as if they were headless hens. One-leg said that we should show reverence to asses for they carried the mark of the cross upon their backs.

I hadn't known about the mark of the cross and asked why this should be.

One-leg said, 'Where else in the animal world will you find a creature with a cross on its back... isn't it more fitting that Jesus should ride upon this animal than for instance a horse or ox, which have no such holy markings?'

The Linguist remarked that all had a cross to bear, what with riots, murder and outdoor relief.

This prompted the man with one leg to lecture us on the different types of crosses borne by a suffering humanity, but he had a lot of sympathy for the carter who had no recourse but to halt his horse in the midst of heavy traffic and cast his waters on the King's highway.

nother evening a little circle of people assembled near to where I was standing with the wise old Somme veterans and they began to sing a hymn:

> *There is a green hill far away*
> *Without a city wall;*
> *Where the dear Lord was crucified,*
> *He died to save us all.*

The wisemen ceased their conversation, presumably out of respect for the good-living folk at the gospel meeting. The leader of the group was the city missionary, a short, plump man who always carried a large Bible with him. He had been to our home one time and was delighted when my mum told him she was saved. I believed he was very genuine and a man who was shocked by the poverty of the Hammer.

Then the missionary announced that Miss Somebody would render a solo, and a blushing girl sang four verses. She looked tidy and fresh, making me feel embarrassed by my torn trousers and tattered jersey.

A sermon followed and I was fascinated by the preacher's eloquence and arm waving. A large crowd had gathered by then, and after the sermon the missionary appealed for sinners to come and kneel down and be saved from their sins. A drunken man staggered along just as this appeal was being made and all of a sudden he stopped and shouted, 'I want to be saved.' I overhead the man who could speak a little French saying something like, 'This will be interesting.'

For a few moments the missionary carried on calling to the crowd to come and be saved, hoping perhaps the drunk would pass by. But no; the man insisted on pushing his way into the centre of the gospel group. 'Save me, mister, save me!' shouted the man.

The missionary hesitated, looking away for a moment, then he said, 'My friend, only the Lord can save you.'

'Then pray to the Lord to save me,' pleaded the man, and he knelt at the feet of the missionary.

The missionary placed his hand on the drunken man's head, and the man wept and the missionary wept and some people in the crowd said 'Hallelujah.' And when the prayers were over the man stood up and his eyes were wet with tears and he pleaded with the missionary to visit his home and the missionary promised he would come that very night after the service in the Mission Hall, and the man staggered off and none in my company knew him and I never saw him again. When I looked across at the girl who had sang the solo her eyes were damp with tears.

6

f living in the narrow cobbled streets was difficult, dying was next to impossible. A horse-drawn hearse followed by several horse-drawn carriages and lines of mourners, all male, filing behind the coffin, soon filled up a little street, and a half decent funeral could bring a whole street to a standstill.

Old Mr Scott was being buried. He was the grandad of Eddie, one of my mates. The coffin was borne on the shoulders of relatives and neighbours. Poor old Eddie was crying like a girl as he walked in the procession; he was too young to lend a shoulder.

As we were making our way down Hopewell Street I noticed Mrs Johnston's lips moving as the cortege passed. She was counting the numbers of mourners as they moved along in slow file. Mrs Johnston was pretty good at counting for her husband went out every day collecting all sorts of bottles and she would count and segregate them into types and sizes in the big yard at the back of their house. It was a grand thing to have a big crowd following a funeral; it showed great respect for the dead person.

I remembered the funeral of my Uncle Sam who had lived in Belgrave Street. I recollected walking slowly along just like now but there had been two hundred at Uncle Sam's funeral – imagine, two hundred, and that wasn't counting the crowds thronging the pavements. *The Long Bar* on the Shankill Road supported his passing to a man, and he was only a labourer. I thought long about that. It was possible some generals had never had such a fine send-off, but then Uncle Sam had been a big man in the Orange Order, a Past Master in fact.

As I walked along I was almost crying myself, for I would sorely miss granda Scott. The old man had owned a couple of ducks and to give them an occasional swim he used to stuff a rag in the gully of his backyard and then turn on the water in the jawbox. This created a miniature lake in the yard and I used to paddle around in my bare feet along with William and Mary as the ducks were called.

Meantime Mrs Johnston was saying: 'Och Mrs Scott love, he had a great funeral. The street was black with men.'

'Is that right Mrs Johnston?'

'It was a great turn out, great. I counted over seventy people.'

'Ay sure my James was a decent man, he was indeed. It was always live and let live with him.'

The procession turned right onto the Shankill Road, then up to Northumberland Street where the traffic policeman – the pointsman – stood stiffly to attention and saluted the passing hearse. Wossie Hamilton was walking past and I nearly did a somersault trying to attract his attention. I had no luck and felt let down for I would have loved Wossie to witness me about to walk up the dreaded Falls Road.

The mourners stopped at a church halfway down Northumberland Street and the coffin was placed in the hearse. This was the spot where by tradition all funerals from the Hammer and the Shankill stopped, and where a lot of men would drop out. Respects paid, handshakes completed, they would stand to one side with caps doffed whilst the remainder started off, this time a little faster, towards the City Cemetery.

Like countless Protestants, young and old, I was in no hurry to go near the Falls Road. Weaned on tales of demonic priests and bloody accounts of the 1922 riots, the rumblings of which still echoed across the Belfast of my childhood, the Falls Road was a place to be avoided if at all possible. And of course a similar apprehension prevailed in the minds of Catholics about the so-called Orange Men from the Shankill.

Eddie and I squared our shoulders as we moved onto the fearsome road. There were kids running about in their bare

feet and when the procession passed by them they would
touch their foreheads and the men would lift their caps, and
I wondered if they would notice the name Melville painted
on the sides of the hearse. This was a sure sign of a Prod
funeral. The little side streets were pretty much like the little
side streets around the Hammer. There were children trundling
hoops and women in shawls, and pubs at the corners . There
was a murmur of talk as the walkers passed by a big public
house near Broadway and the merits of Caffery's fourpenny
pint were commented upon. A hush fell as we passed the
chapel and I was ready to hit the ground at any sounds of
shots. A priest emerged from a side door and all eyes fastened
upon him but he didn't move to shoot. He made the sign of
the cross. Eventually we turned in at the cemetery gates.

I hardly remember the service at the grave. I was awed by
the figures of angels and stone crosses, good shepherds, and
rows and rows of headstones and glass flower-bowls and the
ubiqitous plots of earth. The ground seemed to be filled with
an awful lot of dead people, and suddenly I was scared of it
all and sorry I had come.

I edged away and out through the gates. No one was looking
at me. The men in the duncher caps stood apathetically at
the corners, and here and there some were holding onto
crutches just like some of the crippled men in the Hammer.
But I was past the chapel without noticing it, then running
past the big pub and up Northumberland Street and glad to
get back to my own street, where all the houses had their
blinds pulled up again. It almost seemed like a kind of welcome.

reddie Rea was telling us about a girl in Denmark
Street who had two heads. Eddie Scott said there was
nothing unusual about that for it was the same as a
hen laying an egg with two yolks. Freddie told us there was a
fellow he knew who had told him there was a secret room up
in the Mater Hospital where men with horse's tails swam
around in glass tanks like fishes. The result of this scary talk
was that none of our group relished the idea of going near
Denmark Street when it got dark.

'Her mother takes her out for a walk at night-time.'

'Have you seen her?'

'Yeah, it's desperate.'

'What did you do when you looked at her?'

'I crossed my heart and spat out three times.'

Then Eddie called round to my house one night and asked me would I go with him to Denmark Street.

'Why do you want to go up Denmark Street?'

'There's a woman who bakes soda farls there and Mrs Murdoch is giving me a penny to go and get her half a dozen. She says they're great farls.'

'Maybe that girl with the two heads will be out...'

'She says the soda farl woman's window is well lit up.'

'Are you bringing the dog?'

'I am.'

The two of us were in much fear and trembling as we made our way along Denmark Street to the soda farl house. There wasn't a soul about, and when we passed the dark mouth of a back entry the dog stopped for a moment to have a sniff.

'Jasus John, he smells something.'

'Cross over to the other side of the street.' The dog had looked up to see where we had gone and with a yelp made after us.

'Oh God he's seen the girl with two heads!' We got the soda farls but shot back down Bedeque Street, not daring to pass by that entry. We'd done it. But we hadn't exactly covered ourselves in glory. Indeed the whole excursion had been a tremendous blow to our self esteem.

The following day there was a meeting of the lads. There was me and Blackie, big Eddie, Freddie and Robert and Joe. We decided that if the fellows who had to live in Denmark Street could venture out after dark, then we could. We would go back up. Nothing would stop us:

> *We're the boys who fear no noise,*
> *And never will surrender.*

'We can all bring our sticks,' volunteered Joe. Blackie suggested that we all tie cloths around our boots to deaden the noise.

'What are you wee buggers doing there?'

'What about the dog?' enquired Freddie.

'No dog,' said big Eddie. 'There'd be a hell of a row with my da if he got killed.' And so we stalwart six met when it became dark and started off with our sticks held in our hands like knobkerries. Blackie said, 'Three on one side and three on the other.' Eddie maintained that a two-headed girl could see both sides of the street at the same time, so Blackie's suggestion was stupid.

Joe argued that the best way was to walk single file like the army did on patrol. I insisted I should be the leader as I could see great in the dark. Eventually it was decided that we should keep vigil at the mouth of the alleyway and when we did so Robert stepped into a small pile of dog's excrement and we told him that this was a lucky sign.

It was very cold and dark. No one was going in or out of the soda farl house. All in all it seemed to be an appropriate time for the girl to appear. Big Eddie started to tramp his feet because he said he couldn't feel them with the cold. Joe's teeth began to chatter and Blackie remarked that they gave the same noise as skeleton's bones. Then the front door of the house next to the alleyway opened all of a sudden; it was where Sergeant White lived and he was always yapping and forever chasing the pitch and toss men away from the top of Wellwyne Street.

'What are you wee buggers doing there?'

'We're just waiting, Sergeant White.'

'Waiting for what? And why have you got those sticks?'

'We were only waiting for the monster.'

'Waiting for what?'

'The monster, sergeant, the two-headed girl.'

'You'll have no damn heads at all if you don't get away home. Get moving!'

Big Eddie said later that it was all a move to keep things quiet. He hoped the oul' peeler would bump into her one night, it might keep him in the house more often.

 was having words one day with the nephew of a builder who had his place off the Old Lodge Road. This boy was real posh and went to the Royal Academy. He played rugby football and summer and winter wore his school scarf. And what was unusual for the area was that he wore spectacles and consequently he got the nickname of Specky Royal. He detested the sight of the Hammer boys and used to say that they were not even working class for their fathers did no work. I told him he was talking nonsense for at least we could speak French. Speak it? Oh yes, we were fluent. Specky Royal said this was bunkum for I only went to Blenheim Street School.

'What about *café* ?'

'That's nothing. Anybody knows that.' Then I remembered the greeting the man who could speak a little French would utter whenever he joined his mates, 'What about *bonsoir* ?'

'You don't make it sound very French.'

'Then let me hear you speaking in French.'

'You wouldn't know if I was or wasn't.'

'Because you can't speak it. Tell you what, if a herring and a half cost three halfpence how many would you get for a shilling?'

'Bugger off!'

 always had a love for poetry and my wonderful master at school supplied me with poetry books. So when the Boundary Street philosophers would touch on literature I liked nothing better than to show off my knowledge. Eyepatch said Shakespeare was the greatest writer the world had ever known. I was able to say that a lot of people believed it was a man called Bacon who wrote those plays. The man with one leg said that was just like saying Genesis wasn't written by Moses but by someone of the same name. The Linguist said that remark deserved thinking over. One-leg said that I seemed to be a smart young fellow so he would test my intelligence:

'Why do they have black horses at funerals?'

I answered him quick as a flash, 'To pull the hearses.'

One-leg said, 'Thank God there are still brains in the Hammer.'

But there was another place where I could also hear deep discussions. I went to a barber's shop on the Old Lodge Road owned by Tommy Moorhead, and this man could talk *ad infinitum* on any subject under the sun. His place used to be packed at weekends for tuppenny shaves and thruppenny haircuts and I would sit at the far end of a long bench to be the last customer, just to hear the crack.

'You say Luther worshipped the Virgin Mary, Tommy?'

'Sure I know quite well he did.'

'Boys a boys isn't that powerful now.'

'Will they ever find a cure for T.B. Tommy?'

'Isn't the cure in front of them doctors every day in the

week and them ignoring it.'

'Is it now?'

'Ay, sure goldfish take T.B. and cure themselves by lying in mud.'

'Do you know Tommy, they say that Foster Green who left his mansion as a sanitorium, used to stand up to his neck in mud up there in his grounds with some disease he had.'

'Do you tell me that now Alex.'

'I do indeed and it's said that he cured himself.'

'Why is it Tommy that none of the great scholars in the world can tell a body where God came from and just who He is?'

'Now there's one for you Tommy.'

'Not at all. Sure you wouldn't have the right to call Him a God at all if wee beings like us knew those kind of answers. Stands to sense.'

he Custom House steps beside the docks, however, was the real Mecca for outdoor learning, and sessions were held there every Sunday. There were dozens of different speakers, each with his listeners and one could dander around them choosing which group to remain with, depending upon the personality of the speaker, the nature of the debate, or the quality of the hecklers.

'The earth will eventually hit another heavenly body. There is no escape gentlemen from that eventual doom...'

'Not one of you will enter through Heaven's gates unless you have been baptised...'

'We need the Gold Standard established again...'

'To hell with Churchill. That fella was only a butcher...' And from Tinsley, the Shankill Road evangelist who walked around with his eyes continually looking up towards the skies: 'You're all going to hell!'

I was entranced by the arguments, and by the Salvation Army bands and the singing:

> *There is a green hill far away*
> *Without a city wall.*

Then there were the dispensers of herbs and potions: 'Doctors
had given me up, both lungs had gone. Then I was given this
remedy, and look at me – perfect health and a happy home.
And medical science could find no cure for me! For those
without hope there is a saviour. And only sixpence a bottle!'

'I'm telling you da, you can be cured of anything for
sixpence.'

'I hear you son, I hear you.'

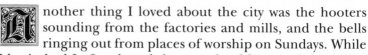nother thing I loved about the city was the hooters
sounding from the factories and mills, and the bells
ringing out from places of worship on Sundays. While
I lay in bed I often heard the sounds of feet on the cobbled
streets; workers on their way to spin and weave. A voice would
call out as someone passed our open door, 'Has the quarter
past went yet Sammie?' And my da who knew the different
sounds of the hooters and if it was Ewart's or Greaves' call,
would let them know. Our front door was always open early
in the mornings – these 'Do-do, do-dos' and 'Woo-woos' were
like a clock to him.

Sunday morning brought the bells. I got to be able to
distinguish between some of the peals. There would be the
chapel bells, then the jerky tones of St. Michaels, for old
Davison Todd the bell-ringer was always inclined to be a bit
anxious; and the bells of St. Mary's and the ringing from the
churches in Clifton Street, all, or so it seemed, helping to
purge the smoky grime from the city.

There were other sounds. On nights when the wind blew
from the harbour I could hear the boat sirens. But I only
learned the name of one boat. About ten o'clock this 'werp-
wherp-wherp' sounded out when the wind was right, and my
mother would say in a hushed tone: 'There's the *Minnie Ryan*.'

Being young I never asked about the *Minnie Ryan*. Maybe it
had steamed away with some acquaintance of her youth. Had
she once stood all forlorn at the quayside watching someone
leave for the streets paved with gold? I was never to know.

here was a man in the Hammer who had a fabulous house. Fabulous because it had an enclosed yard inside which were rows and rows of pigstys. I was in this place on many an occasion, and once over my fear of pigs, was able to stand amongst the dozens of rooting and snuffling animals watching their antics. To me it all seemed so remote and countrylike, as if the scene was miles away from the streets outside.

I soon realised that one could pick up a few coppers each day by going around collecting swill for these beasts. I chose the back entrys on the Antrim Road to build up a clientele for myself among the servant lassies who worked in the big houses. I went around equipped with two old galvanised buckets calling out as I went along: 'Refuse, any refuse?' and of course I always went after lunch and dinner. Mr Kelso who owned the pigs paid one penny per bucket for potato peelings and tuppence for mixed swill, and I found threepence for two hours work pretty fair.

However there were certain dangers inherent in the task. Sometimes a young lad was 'dumped' by the professionals and told to keep out of their area, so I used to bring our old mongrel dog along with me. Not that the dog would ever have saved me for he was harmless, but he looked tough and loved to come, knowing full well that he was going to get a rich feeding. A big lout was to eventually lift his boot to him and cave in his ribs. Poor Scottie died almost immediately and without a whimper.

After Scottie's murder I went over to newspaper selling; although it was newspaper selling with a difference. The evening paper of those days as of now was the *Belfast Telegraph* which sold for three-halfpence. It was a great moment when the horse-drawn carts laden with papers fresh from the presses would thunder up the Old Lodge Road and the Shankill Road. Groups of boys would be gathered at street corners waiting for the paper-cart to arrive. When it did the driver would shout to his young assistant, 'Six dozen for Hooky, twelve dozen for Larry.' Papers would be snapped up and money handed over at prodigious speed, the papers being counted in the way cashiers in a bank would count their notes. And then away all would race like a raiding party of Apaches to cries of 'Telly, early sixth, Telly!'

The assistant must have been an athlete, for when the cart pulled up at newsagents he would with great dexterity, throw down the requisite bundle of newspapers and then jump down beside them and in one quick movement dump them in the doorway of the shop with an ear-spliting shout of 'Papers!', and then leap back up like a hurdler.

Jimmy from Campbell Street had the biggest paper round in the area, and he delivered his *Belfast Telegraphs* around the little back streets with great dedication in all sorts of weather, collecting his money on Saturday nights. One day I was on a free trip to Millisle, organised by Councillor Scott of Campbell Street Mission. An old woman who had come on the trip was lying on a green verge in a lane that led to the beach. Jimmy was on his knees mopping her forehead and holding her by the hand. He kept saying, 'You're going to be alright Martha, you're going to be alright. It's just the heat.' She said, 'God bless you Jimmy, you're good.' Then she closed her eyes and Jimmy looked up at me. He was very calm, and he said, 'Martha's dead.' It was my first time to be such a close witness to death. I was frightened and upset, and though I hadn't known Martha or anything about her, I ran down the beach and shouted at some adults, 'Martha's dead! Martha's dead!'

In a little while an ambulance came and took Martha away and Jimmy sat crying softly on the grass and a few people gathered around him and began to sing:

> *In the sweet by and by, in the sweet by and by,*
> *We shall meet on that beautiful shore.*

However, my paper selling did not depend on papers pitched off Baird's two-wheeled cart. It began at Dunmore Park Stadium on the Antrim Road when greyhound racing was taking place. Most of the punters when they were assessing the form of the various dogs brought evening papers to help them pick winners. When the races were over it was a common sight to see the stands littered with unwanted *Belfast Telegraphs*. As the crowds swarmed out of Dunmore, and providing it had been a dry evening, the kids pushed past them through the open barriers. What marvellous collectors of litter we proved to be, for in no time at all the seating was cleared of newspapers.

It was well known in Belfast that when a newsboy was 'stewed', or left with unsold copies of the *Belfast Telegraph* he made his way homeward selling them at the cost price of one penny. Many a hard-up soul listened for the cry, 'Telly a penny.' On a good night I sometimes collected a shilling, and as for the ethics involved, it bothered me not at all. Who worries about ethics when the tail of one's shirt is hanging out, or when you have to dance about on a cold pavement to get some heat into frozen bare feet?

7

n the ill-lit and at times even dangerous streets where I lived and played I never was conscious of being scared. It is true I had no liking for back entrys when night fell, my mind was too full of ghosts and goblins, but in the streets where I had to make my fun I found some perverse satisfaction in dashing around through the shadows.

These were the days of the lamp-lighters with their long poles, the ends of which were lit then poked through a hinged glass door in the frame of the lamp, igniting the mantle inside. During the day the lamp-lighters washed the glasses, renewed mantles and carried out repairs. One day I was quizzed by a lamp-lighter:

'Do you ever see anybody mucking about with this lamp son?' The lamp in question was fixed to a bracket high up on a wall between bedroom windows. Apparently the man was getting a bit fed up replacing its mantle every other morning.

'I never saw anybody near it, mister.'

'Somebody's going to get this pole up them if they don't watch themselves!'

The lamps gave off a fair heat, more heat than light, and I was to hear later that old Mrs Rea used to lean out of her upstairs window to heat a wee pot of tea before coming down in the mornings, often breaking the mantle in the process.

He made the night a little brighter,
The old lamp-lighter of long, long ago.

*'Somebody's going to get this pole up them if they
don't watch themselves!'*

uring the days of the infamous outdoor relief scheme
many Belfast streets had their cobblestones ripped
out and were resurfaced with concrete. The kidney
pavers as they were called, were fed into a clanking monster
known as a stone breaker that reduced them to chippings
which were then mixed with cement, water and sand to make
concrete. Usually the concrete was reinforced with steel mesh
and the result was level streets, a godsend to horses and to
those folk who suffered with bad feet.

However, the wise veterans who gathered at the corner of

Boundary Street were divided about the practicality of the change. One-leg was certain there would be more flooding.

'Bloody stupid, for the concrete won't allow the rain to soak in.' The man with the patch over one eye declared that he had witnessed the most appalling floods in India and there were no concrete streets there.

The man who could speak a little French mentioned that the Romans were the greatest road builders the world had ever known. One-hand didn't agree. He believed that wherever an Irishman went he cleared the way in front of him with his pick and shovel. One-leg said that the world would be all the poorer because of these new-fangled roads, for road menders had been noted philosophers fathering men like Pepys. The Linguist said there was a French phrase that perfectly described that observation, if only he could recall it.

I was delighted with the concrete streets for I thought I was a bit of an expert at the game of marbles, and the absence of pavers enhanced my prowess. Indeed on one wonderful occasion when I was playing in a three hole match on the old cobbled streets I had a hole in one in succession at each of the three holes. This was a tremendous feat, never equalled as far as I was aware then around the Hammer, and probably never would be. Big Eddie, a dab hand himself, was peeved about this remarkable effort and said to his partner that I was funky-knuckled. But he nearly choked when an old man who had been watching the game came over and gave me half a dozen glassies (rainbow coloured glass marbles) which he had used as a boy. That topped everything.

One great by-product of the level roads and hard times were the tap-dancers, men who tap-danced on a strengthened square of plywood laid down on the new streets. The dancers had blackened faces, which was a vital part of their make-up. Identities had to be concealed from official eyes as most of the men were 'doing the double', and risked losing what paltry benefits they received if caught on. They were wonderfully dexterous. Many of them had fine voices, and they always sang negro spirituals and folksongs:

Away down upon the Swanee River,

Far, far away.
That's were my heart is turning ever,
That's where the old folk stay.

The tap-dancers worked hard for the few coppers they got, and all over the place kids would be tap-dancing upon any conceivable flat piece of wood. It was a great craze and my pals would fit the heels and toes of old boots with sparables, or big-headed metal studs and work out noisy rhythms.

There were street singers too; people who didn't dress up, but wandered around the streets in tawdry clothes singing the whole day long. Many of them were ex-service men, without money and without hope. Sometimes their wives and children would trudge around with them in a sad attempt to wring an extra few farthings from their fellow poor. The police kept a close watch on the entertainers. Begging for money was an offence. If you sang or tap-danced it was a kind of service and not so obnoxious in the eyes of the law. But if there was a funny sergeant around like Sergeant White, then even this service was apt to be considered an obstruction.

But the concrete brought one great improvement. Previously any cart or van coming along my street could have caused the walls of our house to vibrate, and made the delph on the shelves clatter and shake. At times it gave one the impression of an impending earthquake. But with the advent of the outdoor relief work the shakings ceased. Yet, even as a boy, I felt that there was something ludicrous about having gleaming white concrete streets lined by sagging hovels.

It has to be left to the imagination what the noise of the stonebreaker and the concrete mixer was like; and the shouting and bawling of the workmen. It was like Bedlam.

In a house a few doors up from where I lived there were two old spinsters; how they existed no one appeared to know for they had no work. They kept some hens in their backyard and the elder of the two ladies used to call daily seeking scraps for the hens. It was not unusual to see her coming along the street carrying the basin of left-overs, picking out morsels for herself and eating them. It was not too difficult to believe that this was the way they fed themselves. There was a row one day between this woman and the gaffer on the job.

'Mister, this noise is putting my hens off their laying.'

'Off laying what, missus?'

'Bloody eggs mister. Not an egg all week.'

'And what am I supposed to do, coax them?'

'No, but you could take your flaming stone breaker around the corner.'

'And you could take your hens for a walk!' Though many people found the roads less stony they still often led to the poorhouse.

ne place that never quite lost its cobbles, and was none the worse for it, was Smithfield Market. I started to visit and browse in Smithfield long before I had money to spend there. Smithfield to me was the heart of the city, a big covered warren full of stalls selling everything from secondhand books and gramophone records to old clothes, antiques, general junk and keys cut-while-you-wait. It was generally full of buzz and chat, and Arthur Tracy always seemed to be crooning in the background:

> *The night is young*
> *And you are beautiful.*

The books always caught my attention and I would spend hours away from the rain and the cold, leafing over volumes of poems, famous sermons and Irish history. Irish history puzzled me, for often events as related in these volumes would be at odds with the stories in my school books. There were for instance varying descriptions about what really happened to cause a million people to die in Ireland between 1846 and 1848, whilst in one year foodstuffs to the value of seventeen million pounds were sent to England.

But it was poetry that really attracted me and I would always remember with a kind of solitary thrill reading how Dr. William Drennan, the son of a Presbyterian minister and a leading United Irishman, had coined the phrase 'Emerald Isle' in a poem called *When Erin First Rose*.

Sometimes the stall-owners told me to move along, for I

read a lot but seldom bought. Indeed I was down there so often that my father once remarked. 'If Smithfield went on fire you'd be found in the ashes.'

In those days my favourite poet was Gray and I was particularly fond of his *Elegy in a Country Churchyard*:

> *The curfew tolls the knell of parting day,*
> *The lowing herd wind slowly o'er the lea.*
> *The ploughman homewards plods his weary way,*
> *And leaves the world to darkness and to me.*

A few yards from Smithfield, almost opposite Montgomery's pet shop, there was a branch of one of the market's bookstalls. This emporium sold the more expensive type of book, like philosophical works and weighty tomes on religion. I went inside one day and in my half ragged state was straightway viewed with suspicion by the little old lady in charge.

'Are you looking for something, young fellow?'

'I just want to look at the books, missus.'

'The books are for selling you know.'

And oh the lie! 'I'm looking for a book of sermons for my father.'

'And what might be the name of the book and its author?'

'It's *Let Us All Go To Heaven*, and it's written by Black.'

'Black... Black... Mr Black, Dr. Black, which?'

'The Rev. Jim Black, a Presbyterian minister missus.' A very stout priest emerged from behind a sheltering bookcase holding a heavy volume in his hand. 'Black, you said, young man? Now let me see. What did you say the title of the book was?'

'*Let Us All Go To Heaven*, sir,' said I, feeling terrified and wishing I could go there immediately.

'Indeed to goodness I never heard tell of it, Father,' said the old lady.

'Well now madam, there was a Black who wrote something like that at the latter end of the last century. Came from around Ballymena I think.'

I couldn't very well tell him that Jim Black came from the Hammer and had written nothing, but was the only one in our gang who could jump the wide bend on the Forth River.

So I sweated.

'However, for the life of me,' continued the priest, 'I cannot remember the title of that publication.'

A younger man then emerged from the back of another bookcase.

'Maybe I could help, Father.'

'By all means,' said the priest.

'Well as far as I remember there was a Black who was a Church of Ireland man and who wrote a book called – let me see – ah, I believe it was called, *For Heaven's Sake.*'

'You have me beat,' said the priest.

'I believe you're right,' said the old lady. Then the holy man turned round to me with, 'Well young fellow, you've more time than I have to go searching,' and he left back the heavy volume with a 'Goodbye' to everyone.

> *Why so dull and mute young sinner?*
> *Why so dull and mute?*

And thus it came about that I commenced browsing around the glorious rows of expensive volumes, and although sweating after my terrifying ordeal, I was soon lost to the world in the handling of so many books. Eventually I came to where the priest had left down his volume; in fact there were three volumes, entitled the *Book of Days*, splendid and fascinating, and when I looked inside the covers I discovered the shocking figures writ large for all to see – ten shillings, TEN SHILLINGS!

I was tempted sorely, and like that first father of all I fell, for I had succumbed to the lust for knowledge, and so I cast my doubts away. Stealthily I knelt down upon the floor and after removing several books placed the three volumes of the *Book of Days* upon their spines far back in the rack, finally covering them up with an assortment of lesser knowledge. I was confident that the only place where the fat priest would get on his knees would be an altar.

Then began the long hard slog to obtain ten shillings.

'Do you need any messages Mrs Irvine?'

'Ay, would you run to Bowman's and get me half a pound of round sausage?'

'Do you need any messages Mrs Beggs?'

'God bless you son, will you get me a quart of buttermilk. My Willie takes buttermilk with his porridge on account of that ulcer the War gave him. And oh yes, two ounces of boiled ham for his piece.'

I also went down to Millfield to Mrs Irvine's aunt who kept a rag sorting room in the awful flats that used to face the *Morning Star*, a hostel for the homeless. The flats made my flesh crawl, for everyone and everything in them, such as clothing and bedclothes, was infested with bugs. These bugs were universal in working-class Belfast. They were sucking insects almost the size of ladybirds, and smelt like skunks when they were squashed. Districts were regularly overrun by them, and beds were taken to pieces once a year to get rid of them.

Although Mrs Irvine was married to a Protestant and brought her son up a Protestant, she herself remained Catholic and sent me down with notes to deliver to her aunt along with a shilling for the chapel. Prayers were implored for her son that he might get a job on the bin carts.

The aunt was a very determined character, always calling a spade a spade, with long grey hair and a cigarette constantly in her mouth. When she did her rounds shoving a small handcart about the streets of the Hammer she called out, 'Thread for rags. Thread strong.' The thread was in rough hanks and was given in exchange for rags. She was an elderly woman and I thought it was a pity that an old woman had to push a heavy cart and her wheezing and short of breath.

I did all kinds of jobs around the area, from selling papers and going errands to helping to load lorries in the local builder's yard. And so, slowly but surely, the halfpennies and pennies mounted up. And then, eventually, came the joy of finding the volumes still hidden on the bottom shelf; the pleasure and puzzlement of the little old lady, and the pride of carrying the books up the Shankill Road, tucked under my arm... 'No missus, you needn't wrap them up. Thank you very much.'

Shortly after this came retribution for my little sin. My father bought me a bird known locally as a grey for my birthday. It came from Montgomery's pet shop, and its cage was hung up in the hall of our house. Nearly everyone who wanted a pet went to Montgomery's, for they could supply anything from a goldfish to a man-eating tiger. Well, nearly; and the shop was always filled with birds, puppies, mice, gulping goldfish and mewing kittens, and there were tortoises and rabbits and hamsters and great big nets for catching spricks.

I called it Willie, and it got to know me very well. I learned how to blow the husks away from the seed and how to clean out the cage without the bird flying out. But the old flies were a torture to Willie, buzzing in and out of his cage and drinking from his water bowl. One evening I got so mad about these flies and bluebottles that I took a disinfectant spray of my da's and let the cage have a full charge. On the morning my little pet was dead.

> *Tread lightly here, for here tis said,*
> *When piping winds are hushed around.*
> *A small note wakes from underground.*

I considered my pet's death some kind of revenge for the *Book of Days* affair. Sins were constantly brought to our attention at gospel halls, open air meetings, Sunday school, the morning readings at elementary school, and by the stream of religious tracts that were pushed through our doors, a conglomeration of saintly effort which resulted, in my case at any rate, not in peace but in guilt.

f sin was one of the certainties of our lives, another was our Britishness. We bickered and debated but in general agreed that Britain had the best government in the world, the best soldiers in the world and the best navy, and the smartest kings and queens... Smartest kings and queens? Gouldie asked one of our teachers was our present king a smart king? Poor Gouldie! The teacher rounded on him like a Fury for asking such an insolent question!

The wall paintings did their bit to influence this type of thinking. There was a magnificent painting upon the gable

wall at the corner of Leadbetter Street. This picture depicted
the Angel of Mons with dead and dying soldiers lying amidst
bursting shells and bullets. One soldier was kneeling by the
side of a wounded comrade in an act of solace. Hovering
above the kneeling soldier was the saintly figure of an angel
with outstretched wings waiting to lift up in his lowered arms
those who had made the supreme sacrifice. The numerous
paintings of King William, and the little vignettes of the
Battle of the Boyne seemed to pale into insignificance compared
to this particular painting, which I held in something akin to
awe.

Whilst my mates and I were standing yarning one day
underneath this depiction of folly, heroism and hope, a woman
staggered around the corner. Full of cheap wine and with the
seamed face of an old woman on a young body she became
maudlin at the sight of the Angel of Mons, and tears flowed
down her cheeks. She urged us to get it repainted, and to
treasure it and she said God love them poor men and she
shouted bloody England and her wars, and her man killed in
France. And she left us shouting still, 'Bloody England killed
my man!'

Those in our little group said their fathers were stupid to
have wars and there was no way we would ever fight in a war.
And another war was to come and I would go, as did Blackie,
Haslett, Gouldie, Watters and Smithy and the others. When it
was over I would come back without Blackie, shot down on
his first mission over Hamburg, Haslett, who was shot down
over Aachen, Gouldie and Watters, drowned when their ships
were hit, Galway, shot by a Japanese sniper in the jungles of
Burma, Smithy, died at his Bofors when an Italian aircraft
bombed his gun emplacement.

What a terrible, terrible thing, this slaughtering of our
own kind. What monstrous folly. Individuals too, like ourselves,
all over the world, had rubbed shoulders with those who had
clawed their horrific, bloodsoaked way over wastelands and
had come back looking gaunt and strange and broken. Back
to their Boundary Street corners to try and chase the nightmares
away with idle chatter. We learned nothing from them. We
were youth and would not be told. Blackie had said, 'Men

must fight the enemy first and then let the politicians argue afterwards.' Smithy had said, 'My da was a Hammer man and he went, so I am going too.' Strange too and maybe not worth the telling, but I never heard any of my pals say that they were going to fight for democracy. We barely knew what the word meant.

t was well known amongst our group that I aspired to be a poet. I scribbled out little jingles and got books out of the public library like Chaucer's *Canterbury Tales* and Spenser's *Faerie Queen*, though unable to understand much that I read. But I loved the magic of words and this was noticed by my master at school. Mr Smyth had begun a library by bringing a selection of his own books to the classroom. They were kept in a glass case and Mr Smyth, helped by Miss Dickey, kept a register of borrowers.

'Miss Dickey, do you think John could manage *Heart of Midlothian?*'

'Oh I'm positive he could.'

Mr Smyth liked things of a Scottish flavour, and most of the songs that we sang under his tuition were such as *Caller Herring* and *Hail To The Chief.* He would sometimes come to school wearing tartan spats, though it was believed that he was born on a farm in Sligo. And so around the tender age of twelve I managed to wade through a lot of Scott, *Palgrave's Golden Treasury*, and much of Rabbie Burns.

I also liked writing, and when I was thirteen or so attempted the mammoth task of putting down in rhyming verse all the events in my life to date. I was then firmly against blank verse. I had been reading Chaucer, so each line ended in rhyming fashion. Indeed you might say that this book existed in verse form some sixty years ago. It was later to be lost. But as I became older I discovered that T.S. Eliot had insisted that there were no such things as 'poetic' words; and I began to read more modern poetry; mind you, I thought a lot of it was just prose in disguise. The little voluntary library in Blenheim Street School gave me a lifelong taste for reading. I owe it much.

8

n the early thirties there was a great depression all over the place and my father was laid off work. It hit us hard. Buttered potatoes was the staple diet of the poor; margarined potatoes the staple diet of the totally impoverished, and there was a pathetic dignity to be sought in the distinction. For some obscure reason my father's dole money had been withheld and our family was reduced to the latter, and one meal per day at that. Eventually my da had to attend a panel to plead his case. Things were really bad, for my parents had also been served with an eviction notice as we had been unable to keep up with the rent. But the neighbours raised a collection just in time, and the threat was withdrawn. It was a period of terrible anxiety for my parents and my mother often cried, despairing of things ever getting better.

Then my father came home one wonderful day with the news he had satisfied the panel and his money had been restored to him. He said Billy McMullin was the man who had won the day. Billy always seemed to be a hero to my da. In the table talk over tea, that was normally boiled two or three times over, I was to hear:

'Dehra Parker was the chairman, Minnie.'

'Was she any good. Did she stand up for you?'

'She asked me how many children I had.'

'Why did she ask that?'

'Do you know what she said when I told her, Minnie?'

'What?'

'Let's hope you bring no more into the world.'

I asked big Eddie how children were brought into the

world. 'Your ma lays an egg.' I asked my mother if she was going to lay any more eggs. She blushed scarlet and covered her embarrassment by laughing.

T hese were grim times for many men in Belfast. During this awful period of want the government decided to employ the unemployed by issuing them with picks and shovels for the task of lifting up paving stones and concreting the streets. It was called the Outdoor Relief Scheme and it nearly brought disaster upon the entire province. It was a terrible scheme, run by people who showed little concern for the plight of the men who had to dig and hammer all day long in atrocious conditions. Even the concrete was no good:

'I hope the concrete is better in your street than in ours, for we've big cracks coming through already.'

'There's a man I know who has only one leg and he says the cement is rotten.'

Little could match the ordeal those men went through: 'Your da will be freezing son with him having only those mutton dummies on his feet. Take this can of tea to him in Chichester Park; it'll help warm him up. Take the tram. The tea'll be cold if you walk. Here's a halfpenny.'

Extract from a letter in a Belfast newspaper:

It is intolerable that ratepayers should have to put up with the sight of lazy men drinking tea and warming their nether ends at braziers. What is this country coming to?

Ratepayer.

Extract from a letter in a Belfast newspaper:

Does Ratepayer not realise that these men have not worked for years, have soft hands and muscles and empty stomachs? Does he not also observe from the comfort of his drawing room that the men around the brazier have in some cases no boots, no gloves, no overcoats; some of them have no shirts and they have to face snow and rain? It would be a kinder act if Ratepayer could invite them in for a hot drink...

Neither the editor nor anyone else knew of course that the

reply came from an indignant schoolboy. But Ratepayer was soon to find out what the country was coming to. It was coming to a showdown with government callousness and hypocrisy. Roman Catholic and Protestant united in defiance and outrage when frustrated men were presented with cuts in benefit and with tokens instead of cash in exchange for their bread and potatoes from the corner shops. This was the return for that terrible labour.

'Could you give me a couple of fags Mrs McCormick, and mark it down to a bap?'

'Sure I'll do that alright, Sammie.'

Another scandalous aspect of it was the compulsory sending of men to shipyards in England to work there, notwithstanding the fact that a married man would then have to pay for his lodgings and food as well as send home what he could to his wife and family; and this out of a wage of £3 or £3.10s per week. And if he demurred and refused to go his benefit was immediately cancelled.

The people rose in anger. Stores were looted, and although the police were all over the place with guns and batons my father said that, in their hearts, they weren't really trying to halt this uprising of the poor.

But it seemed strange to see a Paddy Murphy from the Falls Road standing shaking hands with oul' Jimmy White, who carried the deacon pole to the field every twelfth of July. And Jimmy shouting at the entrance to Stanhope Street, a Catholic enclave down the Lodge Road: 'Come out and help us! Come out and be bloody men!' Bigotry and sectarianism were briefly banished.

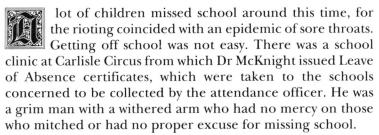 lot of children missed school around this time, for the rioting coincided with an epidemic of sore throats. Getting off school was not easy. There was a school clinic at Carlisle Circus from which Dr McKnight issued Leave of Absence certificates, which were taken to the schools concerned to be collected by the attendance officer. He was a grim man with a withered arm who had no mercy on those who mitched or had no proper excuse for missing school.

On a particular morning the waiting room in the clinic was

packed with children and one could hardly believe, with the
chatter and din going on, that there were any sore throats at
all in the assembled company. Suddenly the surgery door was
flung open and Dr. McKnight, who was a lady doctor, entered.
'This noise must cease at once!' she exclaimed. 'I can't hear
my ears with this racket.' Blackie in a loud whisper said to
me, 'She should tell her ears to say ninety-nine a bit louder,'
and this remark caused me to give a wide grin. The doctor
half heard the whispering and rounding on me accused me
of disobedience. I made no answer for in no way would I split
on Blackie.

When I entered the surgery I had an idea I was going to be
in for a rough time. 'Sit yourself on this chair,' said Dr.
McKnight, giving me a stony look. 'Now,' she said, 'you're
the one with the smart remarks.'

'I'm not,' I insisted.

'You're not telling the truth.'

'I'm not telling lies.' The doctor then stuck her spatula
rather roughly into my mouth. This made me gag and I
instinctively raised an arm in alarm. 'Yes, I thought so,' said
the doctor. 'All liars are cowards.' This remark hurt me
deeply and I never forgot it.

It was confirmed, however, that I had tonsillitis and I was
admitted to the Union Hospital to have my tonsils removed.
The mixed children's ward was crammed with beds. Most
were occupied by two patients, whilst other beds and mattresses
were laid in the outside corridor. None of the girls or boys
minded this for no one was lonely or worried overmuch by
the coming operation. Everyone who had to have their tonsils
removed was always peckish for the hospital meals were light.
And the new technology didn't help. Whilst I was there a new
machine was installed to slice the loaves of white bread into
paper-thin slices which in turn were buttered by a revolving
brush that somehow managed to wipe the butter off again.

Before the operation a nurse led a straggling line of us
through the grounds to visit the hospital dentist. No anaesthetic
was administered, and it was awful to have to sit listening to
the screams of a child who needed a tooth pulled, knowing
you were next. The term used for this shocking treatment

was 'Cold Steel.'

After tonsillectomies we were brought into another ward which was far less crowded. Men in baggy corduroy trousers and the same colour of flannelette shirts came daily to light the coal fires and take the ashes away. My mother told me that they were from the workhouse and lived in old hospital buildings, men kept apart from their wives. They swept the paths and did the many chores that go to keep a hospital working. When I got back home again, I spoke more about the men from the workhouse than about my operation. They made me think of prisoners-of-war.

urvival was the name of the game during those dreadful years, and some of the most colourful characters which I can recall from that time were just poor folk, busy surviving. One was an immaculately dressed man who played an accordion whilst seated in his wheelchair. A cloth pouch was fastened to an arm of the chair into which pitifully few pennies would be put. When it seemed to be close to midday he would glance at an expensive looking wrist watch and cease playing. He would then pull out a lunch box and from it he would select neatly cut sandwiches which he ate along with a flask of tea. I was fascinated by him, not so much because of his accordion playing, but because of his fastidious appearance and by the tiny sandwiches, eaten so delicately. He was said to have been an ex-officer crippled by the Germans.

Very different was the man with the little barrel organ who had a tiny monkey on a leash. After he had ground out a tune he would mutter to the monkey and it would take a sudden leap and sit gibbering upon a bedroom window sill. The man would utter another remark and the little animal would dive down and land squarely upon its master's shoulders. It would then spring onto the ground and chatter and grimace at the group of onlookers, whilst poking a finger at a pouch on its neck to indicate where contributions were welcomed.

Then there was Fusco who pushed a two-wheeled cart around the streets selling ice-cream pokes and sliders. The cart had a metal container packed around with lumps of ice, and when he entered each street he lifted up a bugle that he had slung around his shoulder and blew several blasts on it. The pokes were a halfpenny each, the sliders one penny and the ice-cream was delicious.

Forty Coats tramped around the district with several coats belted around his body and mittens on his hands. He never took off a stitch, even in the hottest days of summer, and he was always in need of a shave. Then there was Beardy Buck. He was a bit frightening. He had a black beard that stretched away down to his stomach and he probably was a Jew. Beardy Buck drove a motorcycle combination. In his sidecar was a large suitcase and he went around his customers in this style with the huge beard flying, selling drapery.

Another figure from those days was Wa Pouffe. He was a desolate man who travelled around with a donkey and cart seeking pig swill. He had some kind of malady that impeded his powers of articulation, for the only words that I ever heard him utter were, 'Wa Pouffe,' which in some way was to indicate to others what he was wanting. One day during lunch break at school Blackie and I came across his donkey and cart sitting at the corner of Belgrave Street. Blackie suggested to me what we should do, and with all the mischievousness of childhood, I agreed. So we unfastened the donkey and tied it to the railings of the nearby playground and then tipped up the poor man's cart. Both of us then ran away to school shouting at the tops of our voices, 'Wa Pouffe, Wa Pouffe!'

Ten minutes later Wa Pouffe arrived at the school and saw Mr Smyth. It was impossible for the teacher to understand him and I and Blackie were most relieved when he gave up. What we didn't know, however, was that there was another man just outside the classroom waiting for Wa Pouffe to finish. It was the ranger from the swings, the place where the donkey had been tied, and after a few sentences with the headmaster he went in front of the class of tittering boys and girls and pointed to me and Blackie.

'They're the boys who did it,' he said, twirling his moustache in satisfaction.

'Right,' said Mr Smyth. 'Out you come, both of you, this instance!' We both felt dreadful and Wa Pouffe started going on with 'Wa , Wa...'

The master looked sternly at us and said, 'Go along with the ranger who will supply you, I'm sure, with a brush and a bucket of water and clean up any mess you have caused. Then come straight back and I'll deal with you.' And he did. Good and proper!

oey Green was a man of a different stamp. He was a carter who stabled his horse down in Divis Street. The horses there had to walk upstairs upon a wooden ramp to get to their stalls. Though he was well known as a drunk, I liked Joey, for no matter how drunk he became he never forgot to attend to his big horse Barney.

One evening I was coming down from Dunmore Park. It had been a bad evening for the rain had come slashing down and everything and everyone was absolutely soaked. I had been unable to get decently dry newspapers and I was feeling weary and disconsolate. Then I caught up with big Barney pulling his cart. Joey was sitting on it with a hessian sack around his shoulders.

'Hi there,' I shouted, 'give me a lift, will you?'

Joey said, 'Jump up there boy and get yourself an oul' sack from that pile there.' I smelt the alcohol on Joey's breath as I sat beside him in the cart. Joey had the reins in one hand and a whip in the other. His head nodded sometimes as he sat there, and now and again he would come to with a start, give the whip a flick and bawl out, 'Aisy now ye big bugger!' The horse would give a snort and waggle its stump of a tail as much as to say, 'Away on with you and sit there!'

When we reached Denmark Street the horse suddenly stopped outside a little pub.

'What's the matter with him?' I asked.

'He wants his drink,' said Joey. 'I always get myself a wee drink when I'm passing and Barney has to have his too.' I had the idea that maybe Barney was a bit of an alcoholic as well when Joey came out and stuck a bottle of stout into the corner of the big shire's mouth. It almost swallowed the bottle as well so eager was it to get the stuff down.

On one occasion my father and I met Joey at a wake in

*It almost swallowed the bottle as well,
so eager was it to get the stuff down.*

Townsend Street. There I learned that Joey could crack jokes
and render a bit of a number. In those days wakes were in
vogue and funeral parlours unheard of. The corpse was kept
for at least three days in the house before burial and
sympathisers would call with floral tributes and offer
condolences to the bereaved. The days were rather melancholy,
but the nights were different, for visitors would stop longer,
sometimes all night long. Tea was handed round and people
would relax and all the good points of the dead were avidly
discussed. Most houses at such times were able to produce
drinks of something stronger and the crack would flow,
interrupted now and then by some visitor who was good
living, and who with the greatest dignity would offer up a
prayer. Nobody spoke ill of the dead:

'He was a good man Susie; everyone had a good word of

him.'

'Och sure I know that, Mrs Bradley.'

'He was quare and kind to the oul' dogs in the street too.'

'He was indeed Mrs Jones.'

'He would always give big Barney a heel of bread when you used to live up in the Hammer.'

'Och Mr Green, he would see nothing starve. Will you have a wee bottle Mr Green?'

'No sure I only came in to pay my respects, Mrs McDougall.'

'Ye'll have a wee bottle Mr Green. Aggie dear, get the opener in that drawer over there in the corner. God bless you Mr Green, if you wouldn't mind; Aggie doesn't know much about opening bottles – no Mr Green, no, no, tea's enough for me. I just couldn't touch a drop.'

'Och now, sure it'll help your nerves.'

'It will Susie dear. It's good for the blood too.'

'No honest Mrs Jones, not now.'

Joey Green then told a joke: 'There were these three oul' men came into a pub one day and asked for drinks. The first one said, "Give me a lemonade" and the barman asked him his age and the man said, "I'm eighty-six," and the barman thought that wonderful and enquired how he had reached that age. The oul' man said, "I always ate brown bread and never smoked." Then the second oul' lad asked for a soda water and the barman asked him his age and he said, ninety - three, and the barman said that was marvellous and asked him how he did it. He said, "I never bothered with girls, went to bed every night at ten o'clock and never supped strong drink."

'Up comes the next oul' cratur who looked like Methuselah and he says in a quaky voice, "Give me an orange mister." The barman asked him to what he owed his long life. He said, "I had about two hundred women before I was eighteen; I smoked about sixty fags every day and boozed and danced every night of the week." The barman thought that was just terrific and asked him his age. "I'm twenty-six," replied the oul' man.'

'Ha, ha, you're getting worse, Joey Green.'

'Davy just loved them wee jokes.'

'He did Susie, sure he did indeed.'

'Mr Green, bring over a couple more bottles.'

'Och sure now Mrs McDougall I'll be running along. Mind you I don't want to be ignorant but I just came to pay my respects – alright love. I'll just have one more.'

Oft in the stilly night
Ere slumber's chain has bound me,
Fond memories bring the light
Of other days around me.

ne evening Blackie told me there was a notice in the window of Johnston's butcher's shop on the Old Lodge Road stating that a boy was required to work after school hours.

'What sort of a job is it,' I asked.

'I don't know,' said Blackie, 'but I suppose it will be a message boy's job. Better get round quick before it goes.'

I got it and began the following afternoon. The hours were four to eight p.m. Monday to Friday, and nine to nine on Saturdays , with a half day on Wednesdays. Mr Johnston had owned a more exclusive shop downtown until family circumstances had forced him 'downmarket.' However some of his old customers had remained loyal. My duties were to collect orders from the affluent Cliftonville and Antrim Roads. The butcher made them up, then I would trudge back round again loaded up with a large heavy basket over my arm, delivering sausages, steak, chops and roasts. For this I received 2/6d per week plus a few left-over sausages and odd pieces of steak to take home with me on Saturday nights. This parcel of free food ensured decent meals for our family on Sundays.

The job meant the end of fishing for the spricks and lizards up at the Forth. I missed this but my family needed the money. The rent for our house in Rutherford Street was two shillings and three pence per week, so my wage was used for the rent and I kept the remaining threepence.

Tramping the roads in bad weather was a nightmare for if it was raining I got soaked to the skin twice because of the double journey. There was the greatest bother also trying to keep the water off the meat parcels for my basket had no waterproof covering; all that I could do when it rained was to cover it with newspapers. Even so there were times when wet obliterated the names on the parcels, and awful moments when I confronted customers with the wrong orders and the whole thing descended into chaos.

 was now nearly thirteen and had attained the seventh standard at Blenheim School. This was the pinnacle of education as far as I was concerned, and others too, for though I could just about decline a verb, I was now seen by some of the older people as a scholar. Indeed some of my neighbours would get me to write job applications for them or to send off letters to relations in America.

I also remember coming home from school along Foreman Street with my books and hearing the odd remark from people standing at their doors: 'The young ones are getting the learning now alright. Look at the books under his arms!' No begowned graduate stepping up to receive his degree at Queen's could possibly have been more inflated with pride upon hearing such words. Indeed it was not unknown for me who had never possessed a schoolbag, to deliberately place such eyecatching volumes as *First Steps In Citizenship* or *Elementary Algebra* on the outside of my bundle of books.

I felt even prouder when Mr Smyth told me I was 'out of my books,' and was to be given a class of my own to teach. It was made up of boys and girls who had proven to be a bit slow.

James was in this class, he could hardly write his own name, suffering apparently from a kind of word blindness that would probably be known as dyslexia today; but no one knew anything about it then. I was to meet up again with him in the future, sometime after James had been pulled from the waters around Dunkirk... the recognition... the handshake and those unbelievable first words to his mates: 'Here's the fella who taught me to write, otherwise I'd never have got into the army.' Mind you, just then, I wondered how much of a favour I had done him.

But there came a cloud to sully the horizion. For some time now a new school had been rising up on the waste ground that had once been Crownville football pitch. Mr Smyth used to gaze from his window that gave a view of the building and say, 'Red Roof will soon be ready.'

Although I had great hopes that I would stay with Mr Smyth until I was fourteen, when I would be completely finished with school, it was not to be. I and most of the older pupils were transferred to Red Roof, Hemsworth Square Public Elementary School, with its quadrangle, fancy desks with inkwells, polished floors, terrazzo corridors and lots of windows. The headmaster, Mr Hilditch, had a private office for he didn't teach, and he never caned girls.

Mr Smyth shook me by the hand and wished me well. 'I hope you get on well in life,' he said, and gave me a little volume of Shakespeare's tragedies. I was never to part with it and read from it in times of war and in times of peace. I was leaving behind me the understanding of a good man.

Blackie didn't go with me to Hemsworth Square. He transferred to the Model School on the Cliftonville Road where one had to pay fees, but as his father had always been in work as a coal heaver, he could meet them. Blackie had got a brand new bicycle to get him there and back, and whenever I saw him riding past with his rucksack type schoolbag on his back I confess that I felt a little envious.

I tried to fit in with the new boys and girls, but it was hard to feel anything like the old camaraderie. Things just weren't the same. One thing I noticed straight away was that the lads at the new school didn't seem to worry overmuch about the authority of women teachers, and it was mayhem when a Miss Jones took our class for singing lessons. When she tried to demonstrate how words should be sung, some of the fellows would chortle and guffaw and mock her in such a rough fashion that on several occasions she burst into tears. Such behaviour towards a teacher astonished me. I had never seen the like at Blenheim School and eventually Mr Hilditch took over the singing lessons and Miss Jones got peace.

I just couldn't get used to my new school. As well as that, some of my chums had reached school leaving age, and had been sucked off into the maw of the unemployed. The few new pals that I made at Hemsworth Square didn't come barefooted to school, and they didn't know the joys of the Forth River and had never been to see the mummy woman. Until then I hadn't realised that things could ever be different from the way they had been. My world had seemed perpetual and safe. The impermanence of everything dawned on me, and scared the life out of me. I didn't realise it then, but I was beginning to grow up.

9

I was fourteen and finished with school. On my last day I walked alone from Hemsworth Square, apprehensive of the future. I remember turning into Foreman Street where the people were standing at their doorways and muttering. I averted my face and for the first time felt strangely ashamed of my books and short trousers. That twenty yard walk changed me from a scholar into one of the unemployed.

Of course I was not on my own. Most of my pals were out with me and we followed the usual practice of school leavers. This was to visit the shipyard and ask if any catch boys were required; to queue up at Gallagher's Tobacco Factory, and to get one's name on the books of the various spinning mills. Certainly there were no discussions on career prospects, no advice from government sources. In short very few gave a damn.

The world that I and my fellow travellers were then struggling in was still stunned by the Wall Street Crash of several years back and the Great Depression was brooding over the aspirations of men like some Spectre of the Brocken. Young men and old stood listless at street corners, little to talk about, nothing to enthuse over. When the days were fine I went on walks around the Old Lodge Road and Carlisle Circus and gathered as many cigarette ends as I could find. Bringing them home I would empty them in a heap onto sheets of paper and begin slowly and methodically to break off the ends that had been in some person's mouth. Then I would strip off the paper and gradually build up a heap of tobacco that according to my thinking was now disease free and fit for distribution to the listless ones and to my pals, for this was our first real introduction to smoking. All that I asked for in return was the couple of pence for cigarette papers.

I also got out my buckets again and went back to collecting swill from the back entrys of the big houses on the Antrim Road. Swill was becoming a little more difficult to obtain; less wholesome food was being consigned to the bins, and more youngsters were chasing it. Still, the money paid for potato peelings had increased slightly and I now received threepence for the skins and tuppence for the swill. Yet it was hard work and not without its risks.

After receiving my fivepence from Mr Kelso and giving tuppence to my father, I went down one day to the Central Library in Royal Avenue. There was a reading room for the citizens in which newspapers were displayed on wooden stands. I was down there to look through the job vacancies column. A curious thing about library newspapers in those days was the obliteration of all horse and dog racing information. It would be some years yet before I would rebel at this kind of censorship. When the state could offer almost nothing to people, at least a thruppeny bet could offer hope.

During my browse I spotted a little advert: YOUNG PERSONS REQUIRED TO FORM ACTING GROUP. I memorised the address and started off for the Lisburn Road. When I was about halfway there the rain started to come down and I ran the rest of the way in a vain attempt to avoid being soaked. What I didn't realise was that the man I was to meet was an elocution teacher, prepared to give lessons if *I* gave *him* five shillings per week. Not what I was after at all!

The elocutionist viewed the appearance of the bedraggled hopeful with an undisguised air of disapproval.

'Have you ever acted in school plays?'

'No mister, but I've recited bits of Julius Caesar in front of the class.'

'Get up upon that stage and recite something then.'

In the broad idiom of the Hammer and in short trousers that clung wetly to my knees I enacted the famous oration by Mark Antony over the dead body of Caesar. A pained expression crossed the gentleman's face.

'I'll send you a card if I want you,' he said, and I was dismissed. I walked away annoyed that the trip had been for nothing. It was still drizzling, I had thruppence and I was making up my mind whether or not I should take a tramcar to the city centre, when I stopped dead in my tracks. I was hearing again the words of *Underneath The Gaslight's Glitter*, and singing it was a blonde girl holding a small child by the hand. I looked across at her. It was Lily Frampton.

She went on singing for a while in the same sweet voice that had blended with others in Miss Moore's class of long ago, and I was back in school with the old harmonium tinkling and a roomful of tough little kids putting their souls into the rendering of that simple sad song.

Lily stopped. She had recognised me.

'Hello, Lily Smacks,' I said. She smiled faintly and said, 'I thought it was you,' and although her cheeks were damp with rain she was blushing and embarrassed. Whilst we were speaking a maidservant came out from one of the large houses and gave Lily a penny. She thanked her and when the maid went away she said, 'The lady of that house always sends me out a penny. She's very good.'

'This is my brother's child,' she told me. 'His wife's nerves have all gone. She sat about the house crying and screaming. Then they put her away. My brother has got it into his head he is to blame because he can't find a job. And you know John,' she said, putting a hand on my arm, 'he's not to blame at all for there's little work for anybody. Would you be working yourself?'

'I'm not. But I'm trying hard to find something.'

'I'm doing my best to earn a few shillings,' said Lily in a half hesitant manner, 'I've got to get money from somewhere.'

I felt a strange feeling surging through me, anger at the people in power who allowed slums to continue, and at the pitiful wages given to ones doing pitiful jobs. All over Belfast distressed folk were singing and dancing in order to survive, while timeservers fawned in corridors at Stormont before the powerful who ignored such conditions. Here was little Lily singing *Underneath The Gaslight's Glitter* on the Lisburn Road, where she hoped to be anonymous in her want. I was learning. Learning from the talk in my street, from the job hunting queues, from the orators at the Custom House Steps. I put my hand in my pocket and gave her my three pennies and I strode away with a bitterness that should have had no place in the heart of a boy.

 was being interviewed for my first real job in Henderson's grocer's shop on the Antrim Road end of Churchill Street. Mr Henderson was a little plump man with a bald, dome-shaped head and a large grey moustache.

'Have you ever driven a horse and van before?'

'I used to drive Mercer's breadvan.'

'Do they employ schoolboys then?'

'No, you see, I used to ride with the baker.'

'You say you worked as a message boy after school hours? Do you know the Antrim and Cliftonville Roads at all?'

'Ay, I collected skins for Mr Kelso's pigs around those roads.'

'Hmn. Alright then. You can start here on Monday morning at 8.30 a.m. and your wages will be nine shillings per week. After six months trial you'll receive eleven shillings per week. You'll have to stay late on Saturday nights and you'll have to come up to the stables morning and evening to feed and bed the pony on Sundays. Of course you'll have a half day on Wednesdays, but you'll have to remember and come up on Wednesday evening to look after the pony. Will that be alright?'

'It will Mr Henderson, it will, and thank you very much.'

'By the way have you long trousers?'

'No.'

'Well I'll see if I can fix you up with an old suit one of my sons might have. You'll need long trousers for this job. Call with me tomorrow morning and I'll see what can be done.'

'Thanks Mr Henderson.' And so I was launched into the world of commerce, delivering boxes of groceries around the Antrim and Cliftonville roads. The shop assistant was a Christian young man by the name of Ronnie McCandless, who went to the *Mustard Seed*, a Faith Mission off the Crumlin Road. In the mornings Ronnie used to go off and canvass for orders,

and while he was gone I would see to Sheila the pony, clean
out the stable, and brush out the shop until he returned
before lunchtime. Then I delivered orders on a carrier bicycle
that had a tiny fat wheel in front over which sat a large
whicker basket which when loaded, with the bike unmounted,
would nearly tip the machine up into the air.

My best run was to Bruce's Farm, which ran all the way
from the Antrim Road to the top of Cliftonpark Avenue. I
only ever saw Mrs Bruce once and that was when she came
into the shop personally to pay a bill. Mister Henderson
bowed to her and saw her to the door when she had finished
her business, and I knew then that what I had heard about
men bowing before personages in Stormont must be true
indeed. I knew nothing about what went on in the lovely
large house, but the smell of cut grass delighted my senses,
and the sight of the trees and flower-edged fields transported
me far from the world of heavy carts and swaying tramcars
only a stone's throw away.

On the Cliftonville Road I used to stop whenever I espied a
huge horse come panting up the steep hill pulling perhaps
more than a ton of coal. I always had sympathy and a deep
regard for these magnificent beasts. Sympathy because it
seemed so demeaning that they should have to act like dumb
slaves, and regard because they did their work with might
and main, and never lacked the will. In the afternoons when
driving little Sheila up the same road, I always dismounted
from the van and spoke gently to her as she dug in her shoes
and hauled the groceries up the long ascent. It was just too
bad if a tramcar caught up with you here, for then it had to
rumble behind until you reached the broader Antrim Road.
Many a driver would became impatient and would stamp his
foot on the gong pedal – to no purpose, for there was no way
of allowing a tram to pass on this narrow stretch.

One day a driver and a conductor were yarning at the
Cliftonville Road terminus when their vehicle slipped its brakes
and started to move off down the road. It was a shocking
thing to happen for with its weight and increasing speed,
disaster was inevitable. The tram raced and swayed alarmingly
the whole length of the Cliftonville Road, tearing across the

Antrim Road before crashing into the *Phoenix* bar on the opposite side. And although the front of the public house was demolished, amazingly no one was injured. The driver got the sack of course, but like the mythical bird after which it was named, a new pub emerged from the ashes.

Quite often when driving or cycling on the Antrim Road a man by the name of Dick McKay, a simple but a happy soul, would come swooping along on his bicycle imitating the actions of a cowboy by whirling a lasso around his head as if he were about to rope cattle. There also used to be an old dog on the Cavehill Road that would run underneath my van with its tongue hanging out. One evening I took pity on it and lifted it up onto the van. It really enjoyed its trips until a customer complained to Mr Henderson and I was sharply reprimanded and told to keep animals away from the groceries.

Blackie, who was serving his time as a cloth passer in a linen warehouse, would meet me some Saturdays and go the rounds with me, or sometimes come to the stable, where we would sit amongst the hay and the corn.

'Jasus John, you have a great job.'

'What do you mean a great job – and me getting soaked all the time and doing seven days a week? At least you can get out for the spricks on a Saturday.'

Sometimes when the sun was shining and warmth was in the days, I would leave Bruce's Farm until the last when on my late morning round. I would hurry with the other orders so that I could sit beneath a tree for a quarter of an hour and watch the birds or rabbits as they fed in the fields. Here, amidst the muted echoes from that other world beyond the entrance gates, I would ponder over why there were so many different shapes and sizes and types of everything. I wondered too about time and space and why there should have been anything at all. All the things that I would have been ridiculed for if I had tried to speak to anyone about them. These were wonderful, abandoned moments, during which my imagination ran free.

f all the roads I plied, the one that I dreaded most was the Limestone Road. It was paved with granite blocks, or square setts as they were called. Even in normal weather it was a difficult journey, with its hilly ascent, for any animal to make. Iron horseshoes found little purchase on its hard slippery surface, and when there was a touch of frost many an animal came to grief.

One night I and Blackie and Rea came to grief on the Limestone Road in an alltogether different fashion. One day I found the lady of a house there in a very disturbed state. 'There's a mouse in my kitchen and I haven't been able to get in for two hours,' she said. I went into the kitchen and started poking around. After about five minutes I found the little mouse cowering in a saucepan, and let it out in Alexander Park. The woman almost overwhelmed me with her thanks. I was the hero of the hour. 'Would you and some of your friends like to come to a birthday party I am having for my daughter next week?' she asked. 'Do please come if you can.'

I told the lads.

'Sure we don't know anybody at all up there,' Freddy Rea said.

'I'm all for going to a party, especially when it's for free,' answered Blackie.

It was a good party. There were plenty of sweet things, lemonade for the youngsters, and a drop of something stronger for those adults who wanted it. There were sing-songs and games like blind-man's buff and musical chairs, and the lady's daughter was very jolly and introduced her friends to us. Later on the woman of the house invited me and my pals to do a turn. We stammered saying we couldn't sing or even tell jokes. But the girls clapped their hands and kept calling out, 'Oh please, please!'

So I got up and said to the company: 'I've written a little play and maybe we can give you a small part of it. Will that do?' Instant consternation amongst my mates. Our hosts however began clapping, and when the applause subsided I explained what the play was about. 'This surgeon,' I began, 'did something very bad when he was a medical student. The offence became known to another person. When the student eventually became a surgeon this person began to blackmail him. Then one day a serious case is brought into the hospital and an immediate operation is required. However the surgeon realises with a shock that the sick man is the one who has been blackmailing him for years and he is tempted to botch the operation in a way difficult to detect, and so end his torment.' After this explanation I asked the woman, 'Maybe you could lend me a few things?' The woman, very impressed by all this, rose up from her seat saying, 'Certainly.'

I turned then to my mates saying, 'Come on.'

'Come on where?' asked Blackie. 'I'm doing no acting.'

'You've only to hand me a knife. Come on now.'

'I hope you don't want me,' muttered Rea.

'All you have to do is lie on a table for two minutes and say nothing.'

'Don't make a fool out of us,' said Blackie.

There was some clapping when a table was carried in from the kitchen and Freddie Rea got onto it and lay outstretched as I put a tablecloth over him. Blackie then handed me a big breadknife from off a chair and I opened Rea's shirt to expose his chest.

'Mind that bloody knife,' he whispered to me.

'Will you keep your eyes closed,' I whispered back.

It was like one of those scenes from an opera when a character sings out their part as if no other soul was on the stage except themselves. I recited a monologue asking God to forgive me for the terrible act I was about to commit. While I was standing there with the big knife held up in my hand Rea kept squinting through one eye feeling very nervous as I warmed to my speech and the knife bore down on his chest. But just at the critical moment, and when Rea was ready to spring from the table, I ceased my impassioned speech and turning to the people gave a bow that would have done credit to Edmund Kean.

Everybody cheered except a bunch of lads who were hanging round the girls. They had sneers on their faces and never bothered to clap.

The birthday girl came over to me and said, 'You were really good, are you going to be an actor?'

Rea kept squinting through one eye feeling very nervous...

'You never know,' I said, feeling almost giddy with delight.
'You were smashing. And imagine, you've written a play!'

Then the party was over and everyone was calling goodnight
and the girls were saying they hoped we would meet again
sometime. When we were on our way Blackie said, 'A right
eejit you made of us in there.'

Rea said, 'Bad enough to listen to your poems, but Jasus,
now you're on to plays and using knives. You'll kill somebody!'

'They were smashing girls,' I remarked, 'and they liked it.'

When the three of us turned into Baltic Avenue the fellows
who had been at the party were standing at the corner:

'Here comes the doctor and his two nurses,' one of them
said, blocking our path. 'Can you not get girls from wherever
you all come from?' Another lad joined him saying, 'Maybe
they are the girls.'

'We just want to get home,' said Blackie in a conciliatory

tone.

'Well then take this with you,' one said and swung his fist at Blackie.

The three of us turned like hunted hares and dashed back towards the Limestone Road. The chase was on and the thump of boots on the hard surface must have made many a householder feel a tremor of apprehension as we raced past closed doors. However when we had reached Cliftonpark Avenue we slowed down. Our pursuers had given up the chase.

'We'll get our boys up here some night when they're not expecting us,' vowed Freddy.

Blackie said, 'What did you bring us here for anyhow? To show off your daft old play?'

'Good job we were better runners than them or we might have been killed,' said Freddy.

I didn't say anything. I had enough worries. After all, I had to go back to the Limestone Road the next morning.

e were one of many shops on the Antrim Road that used horse-drawn vans to deliver groceries. One in particular, owned by a man called Crilly, was noted for its beautiful white horse with its flowing mane and decorated cart. It pranced and danced up and down the road and people would stand and stare after it. I envied that driver, for although I loved Sheila, she was old and getting tired, and there was no way that I would ever get her prancing! Then one day a new pony was delivered to me. I took leave of Sheila with great sorrow. The boss tried to assuage my grief by saying that I could give the little pony a name, and I decided to call her Tiny.

Soon I began to love Tiny. She danced and high-stepped and all eyes turned as she trotted and shook her head going along the road. One day as I was brushing her in the yard, a girl's voice called to me from the open door.

'That's a lovely wee pony.' I looked up from my brushing and there standing by the entrance was the most gorgeous looking girl I had ever seen. She was about my own height and beside her was a pail of milk.

'Hello,' I said. 'Do you like Tiny?'

'She's just lovely. Are you the one who drives her?'

'Yes, I work for Mr Henderson. Are you working too?'

'I work for my daddy. He owns the shop further down the street – the one that has the name Conboy on the sign.'

'I've never seen you around here before.'

'I'm at boarding school. I'm home now for the holidays.'

I was intoxicated with her and came around at nights to her little shop to talk poetry, for she liked poetry also. She would tell me about her school and about what she was being taught and how she hoped to go to university. And when I was told about the subjects she was studying I searched feverishly in the libraries for books relating to them and then remarked casually on whatever aspects of these subjects my cursory reading had fastened onto, and she would say in her innocent, trusting way, 'Oh John, I wish I had your knowledge.'

I never told her exactly where I lived for I dreaded her knowing what my street was like. It would be terrible I thought, for someone like her to come to that dreary place and perhaps say to herself: 'This surely isn't the place where John, who loves horses and talks about history and everything, would live?' I felt ashamed.

At the end of that summer she left saying, 'I love you John and I'll meet you when I come home on holidays again.' I was confused and blushing and said something stupid like, 'That'll be great.' But Conboy's shop was sold and I never heard from her or saw her again, and neither had we ever kissed.

10

hough Mr Henderson, who was of a deeply religious bent and was intent on saving me, sometimes coaxed me to attend the lectures at the Y.M.C.A., I still managed now and then to join the men who stood at the corner of Boundary Street. One night just before Christmas we stood there, the flickering light of the gaslamp picking out the glitter of frost on the road.

'Shocking cold this evening,' said One-leg. 'Wouldn't be at all surprised if we have a white Christmas.' I didn't know their surnames and still identified them by their mutilations.

'Shouldn't be surprised at that,' agreed the Linguist. 'Reminds me of the weather we had in France in '17.'

'Cripes that was some weather,' remarked Eyepatch. 'My darn rifle was frozen up solid, as well as my feet.'

Across the street the door of a pub opened and a man reeled out to the accompaniment of laughter and chatter from inside. A great whiff of stale booze assailed our nostrils before the door clashed shut again.

'Joey Green,' remarked One-leg, but of course we all knew him. The door opened abruptly again and a young woman emerged, moving unsteadily.

'And there goes Daisy Flone,' said One-hand. 'She'll be busy presenting her Christmas presents tonight.' With that the four laughed, but I wasn't to know then she was a prostitute.

The Linguist was a curious character. He would often introduce little smatterings of French into his talk. From what I could fathom he had picked it up from a French soldier whilst in military hospital. But I was never to find out under what circumstances the men had been wounded. I had never heard them talk about such things.

A Salvation Army band came along and began to play carols: five men and a girl, and not a word was spoken until the last notes of *Silent Night* had died away and the band had moved on.

Eyepatch broke the silence. 'Lovely tune that. Hard to believe that our crowd and the Jerries once sang it together in No Man's Land on a Christmas Day. Dear me, hard to believe.'

But the others said nothing. Looking back I suppose their thoughts were long thoughts, the thoughts of men who had clung to their sanity when all around was madness, senselessness and butchery.

A man staggered towards us carrying a small Christmas tree. It slipped out of his grasp almost hitting the crutch with which One-leg supported himself.

'Sorry, sorry,' mumbled the stranger. 'I'm very sorry mister. A happy Christmas to you all.'

'*Bon soir,*' said the Linguist, 'Don't worry yourself.'

'I'm only worried about the wife,' said the drunk. 'Just a wee bit you know. She would have expected me home hours ago.'

'Sure it's Christmas – she'll give you a pardon,' spoke up One-leg as the man gathered the tree into his arms again.

'Ay, maybe she will, maybe she will. Do you know what he did? The fellow who sold me this thing?'

'What did he do, mister?' asked Eyepatch.

'He cut out those words there – see them? He cut out those words for me, I LOVE YOU MARY.'

'Well, there you are, that's good,' said Eyepatch. That'll change everything. A happy Christmas to the pair of you.'

The man continued on his erratic way with the tree over his shoulder, singing as he went.

'He's a happy oul' lad anyway,' chuckled One-hand.

'*Mon Dieu,*' exclaimed the Linguist, 'that reminds me of another message on a tree that I came across during the war.'

'As you know,' he continued, at the end of 1917 I was moved to a convalescent home in England, to a village just outside London, after getting a touch of gas. It was a lovely village, with a copse on its borders, and I and about a dozen more patients lived in this house, a mansion I suppose it would be called. It belonged to a bloke who was probably making millions from the war production carried on at his foundry. He came to see us one time, bringing cigarettes and books. Maybe he was wanting to thank us for the way we had been using up his shells.

'I had been allowed to dander around the district, and quite often went through the copse where it was so peaceful. It was whilst I was passing through the copse one afternoon that I happened to notice a fading carving upon an old oak tree. With a little difficulty I read, I LOVE YOU LUCY 1880. Nothing unusual in that, of course.'

He paused. 'After that, I would wonder about the sort of person Lucy may have been and who might have been her lover.'

'So that's what was on your mind,' grinned One-leg.

'Go on with the yarn and never mind him,' said Eyepatch.

'Well anyhow,' said the Linguist, 'it was nearly forty years since the words had been cut out so I guessed that if the people involved were still alive they were elderly.'

'Anyhow Christmas Eve came around and I was coming in from my walk along this street with its ivy-leafed cottages when from an end doorway a woman called out to me. 'Do you think there'll be a raid tonight, son?'

'I could understand her anxiety for Zeppelin raids were now frequent over the London area. However to try and comfort her I told her not even the German Airforce would spoil Christmas. She bade me goodnight and wished me the compliments of the season and I went on my way.'

'But there was a raid that night and there was a hit on the tiny village. Later that day I was shocked to see that the two end houses had been levelled. It was terrible. I discovered that my lady of the previous evening, Lucy Grey, was no more; she and a baby next door had been killed. What a sad Christmas.'

The Linguist stopped speaking for some seconds. Eyepatch said slowly, 'So that was that.' We had forgotten the cold and the passers-by whilst listening to the little drama.

Then the Linguist spoke again and our little company was moved by his words.

'But this is what torments me,' he went on, 'this is what can still bring a mist before my eyes. On another afternoon walking through the copse, carved freshly underneath the older legend were the words: MY LUCY GONE BUT NOT FORGOTTEN. 1917.'

he story was to haunt me, for such a pure form of love was quite unknown to us kids. We were then mad on 'dolling.' Dolling was chasing after girls with little serious intent. It was not to be confused with courting, or coorting; courting meant then as now, being true to the one person.

On Sunday nights numbers of young males and females wended their way towards the Glencairn Road, not too far from the Shankill. It was a long winding hilly road that branched off the Ballygomartin Road, flanked by hedgerows, trees and fields. In later years it was to accommodate the Glencairn estate. It was here too, close to the road, that the Forth River streamed off the surrounding hills, to weave its way towards the back end of Woodvale Park, where I and my pals had spent so many happy hours.

The Glencairn would be packed with lads and lassies on Sunday nights and as girls would pass by on the unlighted road a couple of lads would call out, 'Hi there girl, do you love me?' There would be giggles in the dark and then quite often there would be a getting together and all would stroll along arm in arm in complete ease one with the other. However, when the stroll was over and the couples returned out of the gloom to the illuminated entrance to the Glencairn, high hopes of having been escorted by a handsome Clark Gable, or being favoured by an exotic slim creature were usually cruelly dashed. It was an entirely random approach to romance.

Big Tommy Bell did things in a different way. A mate of his had come home on leave from the navy and they paid a few visits to the local pub in Malvern Street during the leave. Big

Tommy said to the sailor, who was known as Jackie, one day in the pub: 'Hey boy, the ladies sure give you the glad eye when you have the oul' uniform on.'

'Not half Tommy,' said Jackie over his bottle of stout. 'You could catch the best woman in the world with the bell bottoms on.'

'You think that Jackie?'

'Tommy, I'm telling you. In this uniform you could pick any dame you fancied.'

The drink flowed and Big Tommy was beginning to get ideas.

'Hey boy,' he said. 'What about lending me the outfit for tomorrow and I'll chance my arm in it. What do you say?'

'Jasus Tommy, we'd both be roasted if we were caught.'

'What the hell,' said big Tommy.

'Ay, what the hell,' said Jackie.

And so it came about that a big handsome fellow was standing smoking a Woodbine outside Spackmans the clothiers, at the corner of High Street. It was Big Tommy Bell, and he wasn't looking at the words painted on the sign either which said:

> *When I was a lad I went with my dad*
> *And I got clad at Spackmans.*
> *But now I'm a dad with many a lad,*
> *We all get clad at Spackmans.*

Oh no, Big Tommy was dressed in Jackie's uniform. He seemed every bit the dashing sailor, and he was looking for a woman. And then she walked past; lovely figure, lovely hair and a lovely face. She gave him a long look, and he gave her a long look. He smiled, then she smiled. Then he threw away the Woodbine and walked over to her.

'Hello, goodlooking,' he said.

'Hello sailor,' she answered. And they walked off arm in arm and it didn't really matter at all when she found out about the deception, for they were in love and they married and settled down to a life in the Hammer. My father loved to recall this story, as told to him by Tommy, and told it often.

He seemed every bit the dashing sailor,
and he was looking for a woman.

Sometimes Blackie, Gouldie and I would join the other hopefuls who were anticipating a bit of dolling, with, it must be said, limited success, and our outings up to the Glencairn gradually petered out. Anyway, we preferred the old happy hunting grounds, and the company of Rachel Morrow, Sadie Haslett and Jean Bell on the steps of Blenheim Street School.

Girls from the Hammer, I-te-iddly-I,
Girls that make the money fly,
kiss the boys and say goodbye.

In time to come the tradition of dolling died away from this corner of Belfast; partly because its rowdiness attracted the peelers and finally because of the devastating air raids of the Hitler War. Then the Glencairn became a refuge for those fleeing from the burning city. And whilst the tentacles of T.B. clutched many girls, like brown-eyed Sadie Haslett in a death grip, that filthy war would embrace many wide-eyed boys in its terrible grip as well.

But there was also humour in the streets that composed the districts of the Hammer and the Shankill. And it was this humour, plus the friendliness and tenaciousness, that made for survival. Who on a Saturday night, when out walking amongst the bustle and the talk on the Shankill Road could believe that life for many in the throng was a perpetual grind? The banging of the Lambeg drums and the fifer shaping up like a great artiste in front of the drummers; the shop windows gleaming with light and the grocers breaking up blocks of butter into pats of different weights, or selling pig's feet freshly boiled; youngsters running around with newspapers, trams clattering up and down, and fire eaters and strong men on Peter's Hill: it could be great crack altogether.

Then there were the Shankill picture houses, 'Big Joes,' and 'Wee Joes'; the two cinemas owned by Joe McKibben. In the queues waiting outside them there was the usual high banter from the girls and fellows who had, if they were in a job, more than likely been toiling in the spinning mills and weaving factories all week right up to the Saturday morning.

Of course Tinsley had to be there distributing his tracts and telling the shop-window gazers they were going to hell. And sometimes Gibby would saunter past, dressed up to the nines in high heels and a fur coat, carrying his handbag in a most ladylike fashion. Gibby was full of fun and his dressing up was terrific, which was all that it was meant to be. A cross-dresser yes, but don't say too much, for underneath he's of the tough breed of the Shankill.

And if there had been a pound or two coming off a lucky bet there would often be a party. Alcohol would be brought in, and friends invited. There would be singing and great crack until the early hours, and too bad if the next door neighbours had no ear for music! There was laughter as friends recognised each other on the Shankill, and would stop and relate all kinds of events that had occurred since they last met. Hoots of laughter would often rise above the din, for Saturday night on the road was a relaxed and happy occasion. But in times of trouble, or when a death was dutifully recorded in the daily papers by a bereaved family, or when the horror of impending eviction for non-payment of rent to some unknown landlord was near to crushing the spirit of a struggling family, then tears would be understood and absent friends would join with neighbours and help to dry those tears by door to door collections.

Older men would collect at the corner of Agnes Street and puff at their clay pipes and yarn the night away. Women who for one reason and another were not out on the Shankill would go along to some house in the street where they lived and take snuff or drink tea and have gossip sessions. The idiom of the area was fascinating and could be totally unintelligible to a stranger. A person might say for instance: 'Ah met Tilly t'other night and she says till me, 'How's yer ma?' and I said, says I, 'She's alright except for a touch of the coul, and she says to me, says she, 'Half of Foreman Street is lying down with the oul flu.' These types of visiting were mainly carried out by the women and were known as 'colloguing'. Saturday night, to these marvellous people, was a little gleam of comfort in often dark and difficult times.

11

It's a misty morning on the Shankill Road. The gaslamps are spluttering and wheezing awaiting the arrival of the lamplighter to end their misery. Men in dust coats and dunchers are spluttering and wheezing also, shuffling along to factories and foundries if lucky enough to be working; shuffling along to nowhere if they are not. There are clankings and rattlings as open-ended tramcars bounce along on the metal tracks in the middle of the road. Horns blare from the mills warning the chattering doffers and spinners that it is coming close to the time for the entrance gates to be closed.

I'm in the midst of the spinners and doffers, for Mr Henderson's promised rise did not materialise, and in any case my boss was making plans to retire and to sell up the shop. It had been a terrible wrench to leave my beloved Tiny and those snatched periods of tranquility at Bruce's Farm. My only consolation was that I was now on eleven shillings a week, with no more late Saturdays.

The chatter continued from the shawl covered throng along Agnes Street, along Northumberland Street to Durham Street; past the Pound Loney where from a little house comes the morning greeting from a bed-bound old man: 'Hurry up there girls or oul' McFadden will shut the gate on ye!' It's over the Boyne Bridge to Sandy Row. I hear laughter as the gossip continues about boyfriends and children, or about the film, *The Ten Commandments*, on at 'Big Joes'.

The merriest of the bunch was a spinner from Maria Street. I didn't know her name then but I remembered her as the May Queen of not so long ago, when I had joined the little procession that followed her, our faces blackened with soot and sticks in our hands. She, as the Queen, had been adorned with a paper crown and a skirt made from coloured paper. Handmaidens held her by the hands whilst she kicked her legs high in the air. I was proud to be there, ready to defend her against I knew not what:

> *The darkie says he'll marry her*
> *He'll marry her.*
> *The darkie says he'll marry her,*
> *Because she's the Queen of the May.*

Then it's into the cavernous Linfield Mill with its revolving belts, twisting bobbins and wet stone floors; the bare feet and the over-powering heat. Into the workshops of the masters.

I worked here in the heavy gauge spinning room as a yarn hawker. The yarn hawker carried cages, or heavy wooden crates filled with spikes. The doffers would place fat bobbins of wet yarn onto these spikes after removing them from the spinning frames, and I would load the heavy cages onto an iron truck, then push it down the enormous spinning room, out onto a cold stone landing to await the arrival of the rope hoist to take me to the weaving room above.

'John,' said the oul' lad one day. 'I want you to come down with me to see the master.' Overlookers were always known as 'the oul' lad'. 'I've been speaking to him about the way you can change a frame. He wants to see you.'

I was ushered into his office.

'Good morning,' said the man in the nice grey suit.

'Good morning, sir,' I replied.

'Boy, call the gentleman master,' broke in the oul' lad.

The gentleman smiled indulgently.

'I believe you know how to work out the procedure for changing a frame to take different gauges?'

'Yes, master.'

'And how would you go about that?'

'By working to a square root formula.'

'Boy, always say master,' called out the oul' lad.

'Sorry, Mr McDonald.'

*I would... push it down the enormous spinning room,
out onto a cold stone landing.*

'Where did you find this out?'

'From libraries, master, I got out books on textiles.'

'Would you show me how you would change a frame from
40's to 80's?' he asked, giving me a pencil and paper. I did so.

'Hmn. A boy like you deserves to get on. Isn't that so, Mr
McDonald?'

'Quite right, master,' agreed the oul' lad.

'Well,' went on the man. 'How would you like to come in
on Sundays and water the bobbins on each frame for say,
about four hours – earn four or five shillings extra – what do
you say to that?'

'Yes master, I'll do that.'

'Say thanks to the gentleman,' grunted Mr McDonald.

I was getting on, and I was grateful for the encouragement,
but I hated my work at the mill. Stripped like a coolie to vest
and trousers and bare feet, pushing a truck along a spinning

room floor that looked the length of a football pitch: unbearable heat, noisy frames, heavy cages filled with wet yarn, interminable journeys up and down to the weaving room; push, push, sweating and exhausted, pushing several hundredweight along a slippery hard floor, feet slithering and sliding beneath me. And thinking back to Blenheim Street School:

'John, what is Ulster famous for?'
'Largest shipyard in the world, Miss.'
'What else?'
'Largest tobacco factory in the world, Miss.'
'What else?'
'Largest ropeworks in the world, Miss.'
'And...?'
'And the largest spinning mills in the world, Miss.'

Ignore the fallen arches and varicose veins and damaged lungs. This is the way the world works.

ne evening, walking home from the mill I met Sarah. She worked as a weaver in a factory on the Falls Road, and on turning into Northumberland Street she tripped and fell. I ran over and helped her to her feet. She had skinned her knees.

'Alright?' I asked, holding her by the arm.
'I feel terrible,' the girl said.
'Oh dear,' I said, 'are you in pain?'
'I am not. I just feel terrible about falling in front of people.'
'Och never mind them.'
'It's the way they gape at you.'
'How far are you going?'
'To the Antrim Road.'
'I'm going across the Shankill. Maybe we could walk together.'
'I'll be limping. I'll hold you back.'
'No you won't. We can dander.'

As we made our way up the street the girl asked. 'Where are you working?'
'Down in Linfield Mill,' I replied.
'I'm a weaver in the Great Northern.'
'My name's John.'
'Is it? My name's Sarah.'

I liked the look of Sarah. She had a healthy, jolly face and shining teeth and seemed to be around my own age of fifteen. I accompanied her as far as the Crumlin Road. At the junction she seemed to tighten. On no account must I go out of my way. She was quite alright.

'Maybe I'll see you about Agnes Street. When are you there?'

'About a quarter past seven,' said Sarah.

The two of us met quite often. Then we met at nights and hugged and kissed on the darkened corner of Eia Street. We said we loved each other but she was worried, for she was a Roman Catholic. I told her I didn't care.

Sarah thought I was awful brave, for I would walk down our street with her on a Sunday evening and take her up to Woodvale Park and sometimes to the Forth River, where I would demonstrate my prowess in catching spricks. She thought I was a great angler. But eventually the inevitable happened.

A girl in the street worked in the same factory as Sarah and soon everyone knew that I was courting a Catholic. It was a time when things were tense; a time when feelings were running high. A man by the name of Dan Boyle who was a Catholic publican had been shot dead in York Street.

It was summer, too. People sat out in the street to take the sun, and word passed quickly. Remarks were passed in our hearing. 'She has a cheek that one to come gallivanting down past decent Protestants.' The matriarchs were already passing judgement.

The talk reached my father. 'Listen John, you're going to stop seeing this girl or there'll be trouble.'

'But da, we're not doing any harm.'

'Yes you are. You're doing her harm and you're doing harm to yourself and the whole family. How would you feel if she was shot some night?'

'Everybody's stupid arguing about religion.'

'Oh ay, everybody's stupid only you. I'm telling you, no more knocking about with this Sarah. Why can't you pick up a wee girl from amongst your own sort, there are plenty of Protestant girls every bit as good looking.'

'I don't want anybody else.'

'Then do without. Let there be an end to this carry-on.'

I told Sarah what had happened.

'I know, John,' she said. 'My brothers have been on to me too. They say that I could be tarred and feathered if I keep going out with you.'

'You never told me that.' I was really concerned now.

'It would be nice to go to some place where it didn't matter what religion you were.'

'We would have to be married to do that.'

'Oh, John.'

n the weeks that followed soldiers were back again on the streets of Belfast and the area between the Falls and the Shankill became a no-man's land. Troops with fixed bayonets cleared the crowds from Denmark Street when I was there with Blackie and Galway. There were men waving Union Jacks and calling on the soldiers to go down Hartley Street where a grenade had been lobbed leaving a Protestant with his leg badly gashed. Women were shouting and squealing, and on all sides the cry was, 'Burn them out! Burn them out!'

Then corrugated sheets were erected at the ends of streets and everyone was scrutinised as they came and went. A curfew was proclaimed. Walls had slogans painted upon them such as: 'You loot, We shoot. Eleven dead.' Scores were injured. Fires raged in different parts of the city. There was no way Sarah or I could meet.

My visits to Sarah ceased. An almighty row with my father had erupted, and to make things worse, Sarah and her family left the district. There were no letters and no sightings of her along Northumberland Street; but then the journeys along this street also came to an end. It was far too dangerous to go near the Falls to get to work and detours had to be made through the city centre. I had no idea if I would ever meet up with Sarah again.

The fairest things have fleetest end,
Their scent survives their close:
But the rose's scent is bitterness

To him that loved the rose.

I'd had enough. I jacked in the mill. I wanted to join the army – join up as a boy soldier and get out of Belfast. But this required parental consent. I was very hesitant about approaching my father. I knew there would be trouble. And right enough, when I told him what I'd done he just about exploded:

'Who do you think you are – fed up with the job! The mill was good enough for your mother and me.'

He refused point blank to give his consent. 'If you can't stick the mill you'll never stick the army.' But whatever demon was in me I wasn't deterred. I forged my birth certificate and went down to the recruiting office in Alfred Street. A tough looking sergeant looked at me and then back again at the certificate. 'You didn't make a very good job of this, did you my lad?'

I tried to look puzzled.

'You know what I mean. Get away home now and don't come down here trying to pull the wool over my eyes.'

For all my hopes of escape, for my foolishness, I ended up on an educational scheme for juveniles in the dole office. On my first morning about forty of us were tested in arithmetic, geography, history and composition. A few days later a postcard arrived, inviting me to call with the manager:

'Congratulations Simms. You've done well in your tests. Indeed I feel that you would be wasting your time at the classes, so I intend to let you apply for a job with the Belfast Transport Department up at Bellevue Amusement Park. Alright?'

I nodded enthusiastically.

'Take this card and report to Inspector Rowlands at Bellevue at 2.00pm tomorrow. And Simms, good luck to you.'

The next day I walked out to Bellevue. Outside the interview room there were about six other lads and my heart sank when I saw their nice clean suits. It sank even further when I learnt that several of them had been to the Royal Belfast Academical Institution, one of the best schools in the city.

The interview was nerve-wracking. 'How many three-halfpenny stamps in a dozen Simms...?' Shades of the man with one leg and him asking, 'If a herring and a half cost three-halfpence how many would you get for a shilling?'

'Who is the Lord Mayor of Belfast?'

Close one that. Almost mentioned the man with the Gold Albert slung across his paunch. He had retired, of course, with a knighthood.

But I got the job. Conducting a little open bus around Hazlewood and Bellevue, with its wonderous views over Belfast Lough. And getting paid for it. Thirty-five shillings a week. Thirty-five bob a week – nearly as much as my father earned in McClinton's Seed Mill.

However, I soon found out that I was entitled to every penny of it. The bus – the 'freighter' to the employees and the 'toastrack' to the passengers – was an ordinary single decker with bench seats in rows behind the driver's cab. The conductor clung on to the side rail with one hand, with the other he had to manipulate his punch and tickets and money bag. All the while the toastrack twisted and turned and bumped on the narrow stony road on its run from the Antrim Road entrance to Hazelwood up to the turning circle on the plateau. In the process the conductor was pulled, thumped, battered and choked in dust. And maybe I would have to endure over forty of these hair-raising journeys during my day's work.

Bellevue's grounds contained the zoo, a miniature railway, helter skelters, little motorboats, a ghost train, shooting gallery and a mirror maze. There were times when I had to act as cashier at the zoo kiosks, and it was from one of these that I heard the blood-curdling roars of the polar bears one afternoon. I was to be told later that some visitor had thrown a packet of lard into their enclosure, and that a terrible fight had taken place between the animals to get to it. One died in the struggle, and when I went up there afterwards I saw the great beast floating in its pond, blood colouring the water.

I grew to love the zoo and was sorry when I was transferred from there down to the city at the age of eighteen. I had become attached to many of the animals, though I often felt sorry for the wolves and panthers as they padded out their interminable paths in their cages, never looking or even glancing at one, their eyes longingly fastened on the far horizon.

12

O n the busses in the thirties we had our own little world with its own strange culture and ways. I suppose every firm is peculiar, but I think we were more peculiar than most. Maybe it was the long hours, maybe it was the work, but our little world seemed to contain more that its fair share of extraordinary characters, mostly known by their nicknames. There was, for instance, Bummer Reid, Seaman Watterson, Footbrake Joe and Fire Brigade Charlie, the nicknames indicating the peculiarities of the individual.

Bummer was a born yarn spinner with a vivid imagination. Seaman had been in the navy and for some unknown reason always drove in his bare feet. Footbrake was a bit heavy on the brakes and unsuspecting passengers were liable either to hit the roof or be thrown onto the floor in a heap when Joe was at the wheel.

Fire Brigade Charlie dashed headlong through traffic, giving one the impression he was rushing to a fire; but nonetheless was a skilful driver. Billy Moore was another well known personality, a tramcar conductor who entertained his passengers with a tune on his fiddle and was known, of course, as Fiddler Moore.

The bane of the conductors' lives were the inspectors, who checked tickets and kept an eye on the way the bus was run. The Chief Inspector was then Johnny Montgomery, called Coul Rife, for he always kept shrugging his shoulders as if he was freezing. Another was called Johnny-look-up-at-the-Moon, because of his obsession with destination signs. He was forever staring at them to see if they were correctly displayed; so much so that he escaped death by inches several times by looking up when he should have been looking in front. Then there was Anxious Moments. He was always seen wearing a worried look, which rose to panic if ever an accident threatened.

No machine has yet been invented to match the speed with which news and gossip spread amongst the crews. This also applied to humour. Particularly if it concerned inspectors. One inspector was out examining tickets one day when he approached a lady passenger and her child. She held up her ticket to the inspector but she had none for the child.

'How old is your child?' he asked, as there was a regulation that only children aged three and under could travel free.

'He's still not three yet,' replied the woman.

'He's a big'un for his age,' he said, peering at the child.

The woman took in the inspector's five foot height with a scornful look saying, 'That's more than your bloody ma could say for you!'

Our head bogey man was Joe Black the Watch-man, an inspector who really should have been a physicist for he was an expert on the meaning of time. He was a nuisance to the crews for he would always maintain their watches were wrong and would produce two fob pocket watches plus a wrist watch to convince everyone else they were either one second slow or fast.

He would also order conductors to pick up used tickets from off the floor in case there would be passengers tempted to use them in place of a legitimate fare. He was a man who had a little authority and hadn't a clue how to use it. The unfortunate thing is that if he or any inspector was reporting some ill-starred conductor or driver over an utterly trivial affair, the bosses tended to accept the inspector's story.

However the strangest character I ever encountered was not a bus man at all. He was a driver on one of the old red trams, those open-ended rattlers known as Pnumonia Boxes, and his name was McDay.

Sometimes tramcars, if taken too fast over certain sections of track or around sharp bends, would have a wheel derailed. A large iron bar carried on the cars would normally get the

wheel back on line. This had happened in the natural course
of events to Mr McDay and as each person was duty bound to
report all incidents it was noted that he was inclined to be a
bit wordy in putting such things on paper. He was instructed
to abbreviate and he did so, describing another 'derailment'
as follows:

> *Sir,*
>   *off again, on again, away again,*
>   *McDay.*

He was to vanish after a fatal accident involving a woman
pedestrian. On being interrogated as to why the unfortunate
lady had been knocked down he replied quite sincerely: 'I'm
only an instrument of God. It was ordained that this woman's
life should end as it did and by my hand. No one can resist
the will of the Lord.'

ften I worked adjacent to my own district, carrying
the workers down to the Linfield Mill. The doffing
mistress was often on my bus. On a wet morning
many other workers would also take the penny ride (for it
was workmens' fare before 8.45a.m.) to Hope Street. Sometimes
too the girl who used to boul her leg as the May Queen would
take my bus, and she was still merry and still looked like a
May Queen with her hair kept perfectly in place with a snood.
 I got to know a few of my regular women passengers and
many a tale was poured out to me as I stood on the platform,
next to the bell, after I had collected my fares.
 'I was up half the night with my wee girl. She's got the
whooping cough you know. I'm going to take her down to
the Gasworks tonight for they say there's a cure comes off the
fumes.'
 Or maybe, 'You keep the brass buttons lovely and shining
on your uniform. Is it *Brasso* that you use?' Or perhaps, 'I see
Stewarts have opened another shop down there beside the
Co-op on the Antrim Road. It means a lot to a buddy in
getting a loaf for tuppence-halfpenny.' And maybe a drunk
on the late shift, 'Do you want to hear a good song?'

Many a tale was poured out to me...

And when it came to the twelfth of July it was always considered a great coup for a crew to have their bus or tram stranded by the Orange procession at a decent vantage point. There was no breaking of the ranks so one could sit upstairs and have a great view of the parade. And if I was on a processional route I always knew beforehand if I was likely to be hemmed in close to the banners and the bands. If so I would tip off my pals who would meet my vehicle well supplied with Woodbines and lemonade, all set to enjoy the big day.

Of course it wasn't all standing around chatting. On busy runs like those from the Gasworks to Dunmore Park, it was not unusual for conductors to be literally swept aside before the onrush of punters. A shouting, pushing mass would descend upon the conductor as soon as the bus stopped in Albert Street or Agnes Street, and practically knock him off his feet in a frantic surge to get to the races on time. Conducting could be a bruising affair and the interminable journeying up and down stairs on a speeding, swaying bus, which you got better at coping with but never got used to, meant upset stomachs, aching legs and strained arms at the end of the day. Between getting covered in dust, and sprayed in horse manure, we had quite a time of it.

Mind you this could be light relief compared to the treatment doled out by management. The Transport Department was not exactly a progressive employer. It was amongst the last big employers to grant a five day week, and the bosses came down hard on men for the littlest thing. As the job entailed the handling of cash it was of course necessary for management to guard against fiddling. But they were obsessive about it. Conductors had few rights. We could be sacked on an inspector's suspicion, or diciplined as a result of an anonymous phone call or an unsubstantiated allegation.

However, in time, several stalwarts managed to rally the work force into taking a greater interest in the affairs of employer and employee. If crew members were sacked the rest of the crew were often angered and called upon the Department to think again. Previously we had hardly dared murmur a reply. All we wanted was recognition of the difficulties of the job and a bit of tolerance and fair play.

That spirit of tolerance came when a newer and younger team of managers began to take over. Agreements were drawn up whereby a crew member who was reported by a member of the public had to be be shown a written accusation. This was a great step forward. We no longer had to end reports with, 'I am sir, your most humble and obedient servant,' and the stupid old business of hats being decorated with strips of gold or silver braid to denote years of service was abandoned. Many of the old shibboleths were demolished, and I honestly think that we got a better service as a result.

y way of forgetting about work was to pack a book of poems along with my lunchbox. My reading covered a wide field, and one day whilst looking through a volume of Joseph Conrad's short stories I noticed a passenger taking an unusual interest:

'Fond of Conrad are you, conductor?'

'Yes sir, but I'm more fond of poetry.'

'Ever try writing any?'

'I've written dozens.'

'That's good. Ever had any published?'

'No, but then I've never really tried.'

'Why don't you call with me and bring up some of your writing. I live here on the Cavehill Road. My name's Ruddick Millar.'

'Not *the* Ruddick Millar?'

'You flatter me. Yes. I'm the Ruddick Millar who writes the odd poem for the *Belfast News Letter.*'

'Thank you Mr Millar, I'll call.'

I did call with Mr Millar whom I found to be a real gentleman and I had a most enjoyable evening reading poetry, discussing authors and best of all hearing my own work being examined and praised, which did me enormous good, for I was desperately in need of encouragement and confidence.

Another author I met was Thomas Carnduff, then living in Hanover Street off the Old Lodge Road. I wrote a little note telling him how much I had enjoyed a poem of his which had appeared in the *Belfast Telegraph,* and would he mind if I paid him a visit? Thomas wrote back saying he would be delighted to see me, and to bring anything I'd written with me. My 'writings' were a collection of all I had ever written, scribbled on scraps of paper and on to school exercise books since the age of twelve. He was impressed with some of my efforts and was straight enough to criticize others.

We got on well and he invited me to join a group he had founded, *The Young Ulster Literary Society.* It met in a room in an hotel in Lombard Street in downtown Belfast. Every meeting was addressed by some well-known guest. Over a cup of coffee members would be introduced to speakers such as St. John Irvine and animated discussions would take place on whatever topic the speaker had based his lecture.

Whilst the lecturer would stand on a tiny stage Thomas would sit to the left of the visitor down on the floor upon a chair. He would have his arms folded across his chest, and after the initial introduction would never say a word. Whatever thoughts he had, he kept them to himself. I think that he was scared to speak. To speak would have been to show up the defects of his education. I thought him a most unassuming man who didn't realise the extent of his rich talent. And he never got his due. All they could offer him in the end was the caretaker's job in the Linen Hall Library.

Anyway, as I worked shifts I found it hard to keep up attendances. And when I did come, usually late and in my uniform, I felt that some of the members, many of whom were Queen's graduates and the like, looked down their noses at me. I thought that even Carnduff got similar treatment, and like me felt out of his depth amongst this sophisticated set.

One evening after everyone had left I mentioned this to Carnduff:

'Tommy,' I said, 'I don't think I'll be back.'

'Why?' he asked.

So I told him.

'Be like me, just try to be tolerant of it.' he answered, and asked me to bring my work to his home again as he wished to show it to someone. I was delighted to and carefully collected together my poems, essays, my little one-act plays and short stories. As I was going to visit his house straight after work the following day I brought the collection with me, storing it inside the locker of my bus. Then disaster. My bus broke down and a changeover was arranged by telephone. The defective vehicle was towed away to the Falls depot and in the disturbance I forgot to take my parcel from the locker. But I knew there should be no cause for concern as the parcel, when discovered, would be handed into the depot office.

When my shift was ended I rushed like mad up to the depot. I enquired at the office about my parcel but the depot boss knew nothing about it. I went to the workshop and eventually found the broken-down bus; but there was no parcel in the locker. I noticed that the bus had been cleaned so I looked for the cleaner who had brushed it out. I found him out watching an old vehicle inspection pit being filled in. I asked him about the parcel.

'Ay, them oul' exercise books?'

'Yes, what did you do with them?'

'Jasus son, I thought they were old used writing books belonging to some school kids that maybe you had dumped into the locker off the floor.'

'But they were mine. Where are they now?'

'Jasus son, I'm sorry. They're underneath that concrete.' He looked towards the pit where twenty tons of concrete were burying the thoughts, fears and joys of so many years.

I was devastated. Numbed. I went round to Carnduff's, but I could hardly speak. The whole thing was a disaster and it was a long time before I again put my hand to writing.

I was to write again, however, after I bade farewell to the Hammer, and I was to visit it again in the years to come. But I was lost in the Walks and confused in the Ways, whilst men were standing at corners – corners unknown to me – with their duncher caps and their crutches. Sons of the fathers. And if the bulldozers had removed forever the old tumbledown houses they had also gouged out the heart of the place that I had loved so well. As I roved round this alien quarter dogs barked at me, for I was being greeted as a stranger, and starlings mocked me from the tower of St. Michael's.